"An excellent guide for Type A people like me who want quick and practical methods to manage stress. They really work!"

Brad Aldrich, P.E., Vice President,
Forcier Aldrich & Associates Consulting Engineers

"Inside this little book is a big gift. Choose now to read and heed it, and you will give an enduring treasure to the person you will one day become. Millie Grenough's four gentle, scientific, and simple exercises will give strength and shape to the future you, who will look back and thank today's you for wising up and finding simple paths to healthy body and soul."

Sidney MacDonald Baker, M.D., Professor Emeritus in Biology & Environmental Studies, Yale University
*Detoxification & Healing* and *The Circadian Prescription*

"What I've read makes me feel like you know me, and you're writing about my life."

Nancy Weber, *What I See*

"Millie has done an outstanding job illuminating the reality of the pressures of today and has provided a great recipe and guide in aiding us all on how to develop that personal oasis we all know we need. Written in an easy and relaxing style, this is a must read, 'put it into action' book! Thank you for helping me find my oasis. I needed that!"

Barry Foster, Director,
The Corporate Coaching Center

"Your book is lovely, clear and practical."

Esperanza Diaz, M.D., Medical Director, Hispanic Clinic
Associate Professor of Psychiatry,
Yale University School of Medicine

"Millie Grenough's work is on the leading edge of dynamic health for those attempting a breakthrough into their own inner expression. Her work has helped people internationally for years, and I have experienced her dynamism as both a client and a colleague."

David Darling, Cellist, Composer,
Founder of *Music for People*

"I had a wonderful time reading your book last evening. For me it was perfect timing as I've just celebrated a milestone birthday and have lots of questions about what I want to do with the rest of my life. The book is easy to read and very inviting to the reader. It is full of good information. I was engaged right from the start. The tone was great—you don't talk down to the reader—and the information was presented in such a way that made the reader want to continue and learn more about each strategy."

**Cynthia A. Mariani**, Director of Communications,
The Community Foundation for Greater New Haven

"One of the reasons I think many people will love OASIS is that it simply organizes various thoughts, methods and practices that people like me have been using in a desultory fashion to try to keep sane."

**Anne Tyler Calabresi**, Community Volunteer

"I think I could use your book as a constant reference during my days."

**Woody Powell**, Executive Director, Veterans for Peace

"Let me just say that I LOVE the title. As soon as I read that I felt more at peace. The word alone is something of a mantra, immediately conjuring up feelings of peace and sanctuary. I LOVE it."

**Mimi Houston**, Freelance Writer,
Mother of three young children

"For us recovering workaholics, Millie provides an invaluable service by coaching us to become more effective in the workplace while also helping us to fit work into a more appropriate place in the framework of our lives."

**David Nee**, Executive Director,
William Caspar Graustein Memorial Fund

"How did you know I needed this book exactly right NOW?! You have a fresh, immediate, conversational approach to the reader. You come alive as a teacher, drawing the reader along exactly as if you were there in person instructing them. Marvelous!"

**Lynn Chapman-Adler**, Retired Executive

"I plan on buying your book for others because it presents simple and sensible strategies to create serene space in our lives. That's worth sharing."

**Cyn Chegwidden, MBA,**
Field Marketing Manager for Military MBA

"My most significant teaching that I take away is the concept that stress is a natural part of life. I have been working on reframing the way that I look at the stresses I face daily. I realize now that it is a blessing to be faced with the stresses in my life. My challenge is managing these stresses rather than regretting them. Thank you for opening my eyes to a different way of seeing."

**Sonjia Smith**, Community Activist,
Mother of four children

"Millie Grenough offers a welcome oasis to our crazy pace. Grenough brings her vast academic and personal experience full circle to offer four simple skills that can be applied anywhere by anybody."

**Jane Larson de Torras**, Language Consultant, Barcelona

"Any new book about stress and how to cope with it in our increasingly complex world must be welcomed with open arms. *OASIS* suggests simple steps that anyone of any age or walk of life can master. It works."

**Elayne Phillips**, Theatre Director,
Swiss Musical Theatre Academy

"Looking for bits of balance in the daily chaos? Millie's OASIS Strategies give you short, sixty-second breaks from the zaniness of life – and, as a bonus, they're practical ideas to be happier."

Jim Donovan, *Handbook to a Happier Life: A Simple Guide to Creating the Life You've Always Wanted*

"I use the 3-B-C strategy regularly now and have noticed a definite and immediate improvement as I move through my hectic days managing my staff."

Ginger Mierzejewski, Manager, American Payment Systems

"Recognizing and 'voicing' our stresses, like our prejudices, enables us to deal with them and take action. *OASIS in the Overwhelm* acknowledges that while stress is a part of life there is a need to rest and recharge one's batteries, if only for a few minutes."

Elise Klein, President, Teachers Against Prejudice

"Imagine a group of executives sitting around a conference table, quietly taking deep breaths while gazing at a stone! I smiled as I witnessed, firsthand, the transformation of stressed and chaotic energy into a state of relaxation, calmness, and focus in sixty seconds. They embraced one strategy that Millie offers in her brilliant and useful book, *OASIS in the Overwhelm*."

Carole Jacoby, Master Certified Coach, President of Life Visions

"This reads as smooth as a Japanese river stone. So easy to read, I wanted to read through to the end."

Bonnie Muller, LCSW, Certified Rubenfeld Synergist

# oasis

## in the overwhelm

Beaver Hill Press

# oasis

## IN THE OVERWHELM

*60-second strategies for balance in a busy world*

MILLIE GRENOUGH

Beaver Hill Press

# OASIS in the Overwhelm
## 60-second strategies for balance in a busy world

Copyright ©2005 by Millie Grenough
First Edition   Third Printing

Published by Beaver Hill Press
An imprint of Ludyco International
orders@beaverhillpress.com
www.beaverhillpress.com

The client stories in this book are actual; names have been changed for privacy.

Printed and bound in the USA on acid-free paper by King Printing
Cover watercolor by Randi Parker
Cover design by Elements LLC
Interior design by Universal Graphics
Cartoon adapted from ©Ashleigh Brilliant, used with permission
Photos © by Joy Bush, All Rights Reserved
Author photo by M. J. Fiedler, *Connecticut Post*

A portion of proceeds from sales of this book will go to the Veterans for Peace Organization.

The information contained in this book is intended for informational purposes only. If you have questions regarding a medical condition, please consult your health professional.

**Library of Congress Cataloging-in-Publication Data**
Grenough, Millie
OASIS in the Overwhelm: 60-second strategies for balance in a busy world
      Includes bibliographical references and index.
      ISBN 0-9742368-0-2

1. Body/Mind.    2. Life Coaching.    3. Stress Management.
I. Grenough, Millie.    II. Title.    III. Bush, Joy—photos.

"You can't stop the waves
but you can learn to surf."

Jon Kabat-Zinn, Ph.D.

# contents

# foreword

AFTER A NEAR-DEATH ACCIDENT almost removed me from my busy life, I knew that if I wanted to survive I had to change my fast-paced style.

I searched for ways to balance myself, to find calm spots in the chaos, doses of sanity in the midst of craziness, and plain old comfort in tough times.

I came up with four strategies that I could do easily and quickly. They worked then. They still work now.

While I don't claim to be the inventor of these strategies—they are a combination of common sense and wisdom learned from others—I have developed a delivery system that will enable you to incorporate them easily into your daily life.

My return to normal life after my accident impelled me to put the wisdom into a practical package, a kind of sanity kit, for myself and for others.

What is unique about the OASIS Strategies is that they really do take only one minute each and they really do make a difference.

Colleagues and clients who now use my 60-Second Strategies encouraged me to write this book to help readers like you have your own oasis.

My simple goal is to offer you easy-to-use tools to help you keep, find, or regain your personal balance in this fast-moving, not-always-predictable cosmos.

I encourage you to take a few minutes to refresh and balance your total health—physical, intellectual, emotional, and spiritual. It will not only make you happier; it will make the world we live in a happier, healthier place.

# how to get the most out of this book

IF YOU'RE THE KIND OF PERSON who appreciates background information on a subject and likes to know more about an author before you jump into something,

> begin by reading first the "key words" and Chapters 1 and 2 all the way through. You'll find the root meaning of important words in *OASIS*. You'll also find out what forced me into an unexpected stop in my busy life and what inspired me to develop the Strategies.

IF YOU PREFER TO PREPARE YOURSELF GRADUALLY before going into action,

> begin with Chapter 3, "your story: personal prep." This chapter will tell you how to chill out and warm up before you dive in to the Strategies.

IF YOU LIKE TO GO INTO ACTION IMMEDIATELY,

begin at Chapter 4, "OASIS: 60-second strategies." Learn the Strategies one by one and begin practicing them. If you wish, read the sections in this chapter that give background and relate how others are using them. Then read the other chapters to firm up your rationale for continued use.

IF YOU WANT TO SEE HOW MUCH TROUBLE you're in before you begin,

> read the statistics about stress in Chapter 5, "staying afloat in tough times." The stats may enlighten and/or frighten you. I hope that they prompt you to take some minutes *now* to change the course of your life.

IF YOU'RE THE KIND WHO REQUIRES SCIENTIFIC BACKUP to spur you into action,

> head into the section on "great news: our brains are plastic" in Chapter 5. I recommend this section particularly for those of you who may be skeptical about anything that appears to be "touchy-feely." With Type A personality engineers and CEOs, I usually lead off with this information; new developments in brain research intrigue and motivate them.

Whichever way you use OASIS, remember that the best way—in fact, the only way—to make it work is to use the book as a guide to action.

Do it.

I promise you that:

- you can learn all four OASIS Strategies in one hour or less,
- you can use them immediately in your daily life at work and at home,
- they will make a positive difference in your life, and
- people around you will be glad you are using them.

# key words

WORDS SUCH AS CRAZY AND SANE float through our daily conversations, often without us giving them a second thought. The root derivations of these words might sharpen your understanding as you prepare to use the four OASIS Strategies.

I include below four words from the book's title: *balance, oasis, overwhelm* and *strategy*. Regarding other key words, I hope that *OASIS* will encourage you to nourish the neuroplasticity of your brain to provide both sanity and refuge when craziness threatens to overwhelm.

**balance** Latin [*bi*]+ [*lanx*], having two scale-pans; 1. equipoise between contrasting, opposing, or interacting elements

**crazy** Middle English [*crazen*], to break, break in pieces; 1. unsound, cracked, shaky, rickety; 2. mentally unbalanced or deranged

**neuroplasticity** Greek [*neuro*], nerve, sinew + [*plassein*], to mold, form; 1. the ability of the brain to develop throughout life

**oasis** Late Latin from Greek [*oasis*], a fertile spot; originally Coptic: fertile land in the Libyan desert; 1. a fertile place in a desert where water

may be found; 2. a place of refuge or time of
refuge

**overwhelm**\* Middle English [*over*], over +
[*whelmen*] to turn over, cover up; 1. to
overpower in thought or feeling
*\*Prompted by my client Kathy, I use "overwhelm"
in this book as a noun.*

**refuge** Latin [*refugium: re-*], back, and [*fugere*], to
flee; 1. shelter from danger or distress; 2. a place
of safety

**sanity** Latin [*sanitas*], health: from [*sanus*], sound,
whole; 1. ability to anticipate and appraise the
effect of one's actions; 2. condition of being free
from hurt or disease: healthy

**strategy** Greek [*strategia*], generalship; 1. the art of
devising plans or stratagems towards a goal

chapter 1

# the overwhelm

"I'D LIKE TO DO THAT but I just don't have the time or energy."

"I'd love to slow down but I'm a Type A personality. I'm afraid if I let up, I'll lose my drive."

"I can't ever catch up."

"My life . . . My desk . . . My kids . . . My closet . . . My weight . . . My health . . . My finances . . . The world . . . is in such a mess now, I don't know where to start. And you know what? I think it's getting worse.'

Sound familiar?

For over three decades, I've heard complaints like these from the smart, busy people I work with.

These days I notice something different. The women and men who pass through my office door today carry a ground-level malaise—an increased sense of urgency—that was not present a few years back. They're looking for some kind of balance in a world that is increasingly topsy-turvy. They want refuge. As about-to-be fifty Kathy says,

"There's way too much to deal with. I'm lost in the overwhelm."

Our times are intense and turbulent. And, thanks to the sophistication of our media, the colors, sounds, and minute details are in our face daily. Headlines, picayune and profound, vie for our attention. Illusory promises such as "Tight abs in six days" or "Lose forty pounds in two weeks" compete with shocking news of neighborhood murders. Twenty-four-hour TV displays increasingly spectacular ways to assuage our agitation: "Buy your dream house with no money down" and "Visit exotic places you've only seen in travel magazines" accompany news about the latest terrorist attacks in those exotic locales.

Medical science announces incredible advances, yet the findings often leave us more confused about whether it's safe or dangerous to take the latest drug. Monthly magazines promote trendy labor-efficient devices. We buy them and get busier trying to make them work.

Even school kids are stretched thin. When I finally caught up with my thirteen-year-old niece to make a date with her, she said,

"Not this week or next, Mil. I've got something every day after school. Then I'm tied up all weekend. Maybe the week after that?"

## when do we get a break?

AH, YES, VACATION. But we wonder if we will get there without a hitch and if the spot will be safe. When we finally arrive, we're often sick the first few days because we crammed in so much activity to prep for getting away. Mid-vacation we begin to worry about everything we need to do when we return. Or we're already trying to handle it. After tax season last year, my accountant Ron went to Key West for a week to get away from it all. He said he couldn't relax because everybody else at the swimming pool was glued either to their laptops or their cell phones.

It doesn't seem to matter what your age, gender, or profession is, whether you're the owner of your own business or an employee, retired or looking for work, whether you have kids or are childless, have a significant relationship or none, have lots of money or only a little. Whether you're CEO of a corporation, CEO of your family, or simply the CEO of your life, times are tough. And they're not getting any easier.

Outside pressures and our own expectations multiply even as our available time and energy to deal with life's ups and downs keep shrinking. Events that we have little personal control over—violence, terrorism, the environment, the economy—catch us in their whirl. Our ability to manage these realities seems to be ever more elusive.

### gimme shelter

WISH YOU COULD FIND A WAY TO STAY SANE in the midst of all the anxiety? You're not alone. Many of us, and I include myself, aren't entirely happy about how we're using the precious moments of our lives. Allison, a well-respected university professor in her thirties, tells me,

> "I wish I felt better about my accomplishments. I used to love what I do, but I'm losing my enthusiasm for it. I rarely feel satisfied. I feel like I'm always dealing with details, chasing after something that's not there. I don't want to get into my fifties, look back and say 'Geez, why didn't I recognize then all that I had going for me and enjoy it?'"

Forty-five-year-old engineer Mark says,

> "I've finally reached where I want to be professionally. Only trouble is, with all the pressures on me at work, I don't have much time for my kids. They're teenagers already. My work and my

family are important to me. I can't figure out a way to be okay with both of them. Besides all that, I'm really worried about what the world's going to be like when my kids grow up."

Working mom Patti sighs,

"In the morning, when the twins are going bonkers and my husband needs something and I'm still not ready to go to work, I'm almost over the edge. There are just too many things to worry about. My mom's health is deteriorating. My husband isn't sure his job is going to be here next month. And my kids are having nightmares about terrorists coming into our neighborhood. I have trouble sleeping, too, so it's really hard for me to concentrate at work."

When I ask Patti how she and her husband are getting along, she replies,

"Oh, that's another pressure. He wants sex. Who's got time or energy for that?"

### more anxiety, less control

IN THESE DAYS OF INCREASED PRESSURE, our systems are in a constant state of alert without us even realizing it.

Dr. Robert M. Sapolsky, in his book *Why Zebras Don't Get Ulcers*, explains that animals make much better use of their lifesaving stress responses than most of us humans do. Rather than turning our stress responses on and off as needed, we humans plug into them with extravagant frequency: when we are sitting frustrated in traffic jams, worrying about expenses, mulling over tense interactions with colleagues, or even trying to find a quarter that we dropped on the floor of the car. Sapolsky says that if we can't *turn on* a stress response when it's needed— as an animal does when it runs away from a hungry lion—we're in trouble. But even more,

> "If you repeatedly *turn on* the stress response, or if you cannot appropriately *turn off* the stress response at the end of a stressful event, the stress response can eventually become nearly as damaging as some stressors themselves."[1]

Medical experts say that we live now in a "chronic heightened state of alertness accompanied by an increased sense of helplessness."[2] Simply stated, our lives are more complex and our world is less predictable and more dangerous than it used to be. In response to this state of affairs, our stress responses are going berserk. As Sapolsky remarks,

> "If your blood pressure rises to 180/120 when

lifetime, he might have thought it was a laxative or maybe something to keep his Ford going. At the end of his long workday, Dad usually unwound by sitting on the front porch. And almost every Sunday he took us and a bunch of neighborhood kids down to Shawnee Park where we could see the Indiana farmlands from our Louisville side of the Ohio River. He sat by the river while we ran up and down the hills.

The tempo has quickened since my Dad was around. Schedules are more packed. Responsibilities seem never to end. My OASIS Strategies recognize that reality. I have shaped them for people who don't have time.

- You can learn the Strategies in less than an hour.
- Each of the four Strategies takes only 60 seconds to use.

If you can't clear that much space for yourself and your peace of mind, you may as well stop reading now.

Just a minute.

Honest.

That's all it takes.

About that 24/7, my friend Jane says:

> "Sure, we all live 24/7 lives. No doubt about it. The real question is, 'What do you want those twenty-four hours and seven days to be?'"

You do have a choice.

chapter 2

# my story: why I wrote this book

LIKE MANY OF MY CLIENTS AND COLLEAGUES, I am ambitious and somewhat driven. And like many people I know, I am pretty bullheaded. It took a near-death accident to make me alter my fast-paced daily routine.

I spent the first decades of my life on three continents. I grew up the fifth of seven kids in a Kentucky working-class family. Neighbors called our house "the one with the swinging doors." Our single-bath home somehow accommodated the short and long stays of assorted ill relatives, neighborhood kids looking for companionship, and students from other countries. The visitors from Latin America and Asia especially intrigued me. I was eager to know more about what made them tick.

The month after my college graduation I remember standing in our backyard asking myself:

"Okay, Mil, what will it be: two years for John F. Kennedy and the USA, or your whole life for God and the whole world?"

I aimed for what I then thought was the highest, the best. The Maryknoll Sisters beat out the Peace Corps.

My eight years as a Catholic nun taught me much about discipline and caring for others. And they brought me to Latin America. The experiences there with wonderful, warm Mexicans and Panamanians, Bolivians and Peruvians opened me to a deeper realization of my mission. I realized that I did not want to be celibate all my life and I knew that I needed to find a way to let music be a bigger part of my expression in the world.

I left the convent and began a fresh life in the USA. I found a bass fiddle teacher, got a job teaching English to adults from fifteen countries, and began dating for the first time in my life. I then went to Europe for three years to study music, learn more about other cultures, and try out new ways of teaching English. Gradually, I let go of my shyness. When I returned to the States, I began to follow my passions with more determination. I became a night-club singer, body/mind therapist, award-winning author, and international workshop presenter.

Along the way I took a trip to Nicaragua, learned more scintillating Latino songs, and met the man who would become my husband.

I was cruising along quite happily. I married the sweet guy, semi-inherited three lively teenage boys in the process, launched my own business, and was poised to complete a new version of my textbook-cassette series.

Cruising along probably isn't the most accurate phrase. It was more like running at breakneck speed.

### stop

ON A CLEAR, BRIGHT SUNDAY MORNING IN JULY, my friend Joe phoned to ask if I wanted to go for a bike ride. As usual, I had five events already lined up for that day, but I thought, "What the heck? It's such a gorgeous day. I can squeeze this in."

I hoisted my ten-speed onto my Camry and drove out to meet Joe at a great biking spot an hour out of New Haven. We grabbed a sandwich in the Deep River town market and then headed out for the river country.

As we raced up and down rolling hills, a small pothole suddenly brought me to a stop, almost a dead stop. It flipped me over the handlebars, threw me to the pavement, and left me unconscious in the middle of the rural road.

My biking companion later told me:

"For what seemed like a long time, you didn't move. I thought you were dead. I was terrified. Then you had a convulsion and blood came out of your mouth. I was afraid you'd be a vegetable all your life."

No help nearby. No cellphone. Finally, a couple in a car passed. They drove into town and called for help.

A Life Star helicopter flew me to the Yale-New Haven Hospital emergency room. During the forty-two mile trip, I came to consciousness only once, long enough to hear the whirr of the helicopter blade and to feel the hands of the paramedic cradling my head. "She's good," I remember thinking as I slid back under.

### surreal

I WAKE TO BRIGHT LIGHTS, LOUD NOISES . . . E.R . . . lots of people, all strangers . . .

I hear myself say, "Hand . . . hand . . . ," then unconscious. Lights and noise again. "Hand . . . hand . . ." No response. Under again. Up . . . "Hand . . ." Maybe this time they'll hear me.

Awake . . . There's a young woman standing next to me. Something's touching my hand . . . the candy

striper is holding my hand . . . but it feels funny. . . .
Oh . . . she's wearing rubber gloves. I hear myself say,
"Skin . . . skin. . . ." Under again.

The next few days are a blur. I recall drifting in
and out of consciousness frequently. I remember a
morning when I spotted white-coated beings with
clipboards circling my bed. . . . I heard the most
official-looking white coat say,

"Female, bicycle accident, three concussions,
ruptured kidney."

That must be me. . . . I look up. . . . No one seems
to notice. . . . Under again. . . . Sometime later, it's
dark. I guess it's night. . . . A movement near my
head rouses me. . . . The movement feels soft, and
there is soft singing near it. . . . The softness is
mopping the floor, straightening my table. . . . Then
it says,

"How you doin', honey?" and lightly brushes
hair off my forehead.

## outdoor rehab

AFTER MY RELEASE FROM THE HOSPITAL, the slow, surreal pace continued—no choice about it. For the first few weeks, my most strenuous activity was laying in my backyard hammock. Gradually I advanced to watching the ants move under the picnic table.

For the first time in a long time I had a chance to look at the really big questions:

Who am I?
What on earth am I here for?

The rhododendrons at the right side of the hammock progressed, very slowly, from tight buds to gloriously open blossoms. The questions danced around:

Who am I, really?

And what the heck am I on this earth for?

As my eyes followed the picnic-table ants moving so purposefully, I stayed close to the questions.

I began to play around with strategies to bring myself back to health. The going was slow, but the direction was true.

I knew that I *would* get better. I also knew that when I left the hammock and returned to *normal* life, I'd be tempted to get into the fast lane again. After all, the rat race has its appeal. It's exciting and appears to be going somewhere. Besides, there are lots of other interesting rats running along with me. I realized that I could be sucked in quite easily.

The doctors, nurses, and technicians in the hospital had taken excellent care of me or else I wouldn't be alive today. I was extremely grateful for their expertise. But there was something missing in their care for me, some vital juice.

I recalled that in those first surreal days the only person who called me by name was an orderly. He must have looked at the hospital bracelet on my wrist after I fainted in the X-ray room. I awakened to him saying "Mildred . . . Mildred. . . ." He was holding my hand, no rubber gloves. I remember thinking, "Thank God. There's a human being here!" before I lost consciousness again.

Before my accident I had worked in the mental health division of the same hospital. I knew what it was like to deal with patients in crisis and then be swamped with paperwork. Now that I had been on the opposite side, I wondered: Had my patients felt as unseen as I had? Had I been so expert at my job, so focused on the diagnosis, that I had missed the face of the person in front of me?

### promises

BEFORE I LEFT THE HAMMOCK IN MY BACKYARD, I made two promises to myself:

1. I'd find specific strategies for myself to live a saner, more balanced life.

2. If the strategies worked for me, I'd find ways to share them with my harried colleagues.

I realized that I would need practical things that I could do every day, actions that wouldn't interfere with my life, but that might even make it easier and more enjoyable. I wanted practices that would affect my overall health, would help me to be more effective in my work and more loving to myself and to others. I searched for simple tools that would help me keep my balance even when things got really crazy.

I began experimenting. I figured that if I found some techniques that worked for me, they'd have a good chance of working for other busy, driven people.

I decided that whatever techniques I settled on had to meet the following criteria:

✓ easy to learn
✓ simple and quick to do
✓ medically and psychologically sound
✓ immediately effective and offer long-range benefits
✓ directed to total, not simply one aspect of, health (by total health, I mean physical, intellectual, emotional, and spiritual health)
✓ useful for people of various ages and lifestyles
✓ inexpensive, or preferably free, and
✓ enjoyable enough that once people had done them, they would want to do them again.

Furthermore, the strategies would not necessitate:

✓ joining a gym or hiring a personal trainer
✓ making major life changes, e.g. quitting a job, divorcing, evicting the kids, moving to Hawaii.

Very gradually, I developed four strategies that met the criteria. The Strategies were straightforward, practical, and doable. I used them. They worked.

When I was on my feet again, I began conducting *Self-Care for Caregivers* workshops. If we service providers didn't learn how to take care of ourselves, I knew that we wouldn't be much help to the people around us. And we'd burn ourselves out.

I taught the Strategies to my colleagues: therapists, hospice nurses, doctors. They worked. Word spread. Front-line managers at homeless shelters, daycare guardians, grandparents raising grandchildren asked for them, began using them, and continued to use them.

Perhaps because I was so focused on my colleagues, it took me a while to realize that caregivers aren't the only ones who are stretched. One day, my accountant Ron said,

"Millie, your human services crowd doesn't have a monopoly on this. We business people want the same things you want—a sense that we're doing something that's valuable for our clients, time for ourselves, quality time with our families—some kind of balance."

He added,

"We're out there in the world dealing with competition and bottom line issues every minute. We need a break, too."

Ron and I made a date for lunch. He showed up with his business partner who said he was "really stressed out." Before we finished dessert, I had taught both of them two of the OASIS Strategies. They absorbed them and wanted more.

## post-hammock

I'VE BEEN IN REAL LIFE for quite a while now. I'm doing my best to take better care of myself. And I've taught the 60-Second Strategies to hundreds of people: CEOs and other business professionals, attorneys, telephone operators, prison inmates, athletes, graduate students, university deans, fifth-graders, clergy, five-year olds, parents, grandparents, artists, and salespeople.

When I was in the hospital recovering from my cranial injuries, I had a vague notion that my brain and my mind were operating in a manner different from before. However, I had no idea that concurrent research was exploring the multiple ways in which the brain changes, even when it has not been affected by an accident.

As I presented my strategies to wider audiences, I learned more about developments in neuro-psychiatry and brain research. I was incredibly excited by these new findings. I knew that the day-to-day experiences I was having in the field with my clients were in sync with the research findings: people who used the Strategies on a regular basis were indeed changing their brains and their bodies. And in doing this, they were improving their health and happiness.

I was thrilled that the new findings gave scientific backing to my techniques. I began to incorporate the new research about the brain's neuroplasticity into my workshops. Skeptics were convinced. Hardnosed realists learned the Strategies and used them. It was the first time that they had found practical, efficient one-minute actions that could change their lives, and that had the validation of scientific research.

After he learned the OASIS Strategies, CEO Nick wrote to me,

"I want you to know how much I appreciate the difference the Strategies have made in my life. I use those tools daily."

Jessica, a stay-at-home mom, said,

"They really help me—and my son—cool down."

After a 60-Second Strategies workshop, Sarah, Vice President of Operations in a large non-profit organization, wrote me,

> "They're so very helpful and, best of all, so very doable. These are suggestions that can easily be turned into action by the busiest of us."

The OASIS Strategies provided quick, practical medicine. Workshop participants asked me for written descriptions to pass along to their co-workers and relatives. Clients and colleagues urged me to combine my Strategies and the new brain research into a practical, readable book that would be useful for people from all walks of life. *OASIS in the Overwhelm* is my response.

chapter 3

# your story: personal prep

"THE MOST POWERFUL—and the most controllable—stressor in the world is the human mind."[1]

So, what would you rather have: pain or pleasure? This very minute, what's your choice? If you chose pain, you're reading the wrong book. If you opted for pleasure, get ready to better your balance.

This chapter leads you through three steps to prepare yourself for the Strategies.

A gentle reminder: this is definitely a do-it-yourself book. The OASIS Strategies can change your life dramatically. But there won't be any miracles unless you perform them. As the Chinese proverb says,

Tell me, I'll forget.
Show me, I may remember.
Involve me, and I'll understand.

## chill out

FIND A RESTFUL PLACE TO SIT DOWN. Have paper and pen handy. Prepare yourself to *actively* chill out. If you're more relaxed with your shoes off, shed them. Loosen your belt. Loosen your mind.

- Give yourself the opportunity to take a few delicious, non-pressured breaths. As you inhale, feel the breath move gently through your nostrils. Let the breath find its way down through your throat and chest and down to your stomach. Feel your stomach expand as the breath enters.

- Then, as you release the breath, sense how your stomach relaxes, eases. Enjoy the feeling of the breath floating out through your nostrils. Notice how, when you take really conscious breaths, you remember that you have a body as well as a mind.

- Lengthen your legs, your arms, your whole torso. Let your spine have lots of space.

- Turn your head slowly from left to right. Let your eyes take in whatever is around you. Then let that view go.

- Come back to your breath and your book. Let yourself settle into your fresh place of balance.

By doing this brief debrief, you're already shaking off dead energy and resetting your equilibrium.

## warm up

NOW THAT YOUR MIND AND BODY ARE CLEARER, you're ready to focus your intention. Take time now to ask yourself:

**Question #1:**
**At this precise moment in my life, what are my toughest challenges/problems/ stressors?**

Pinpoint *your* current personal realities. Include your health, your work, your family, your financial status, your thoughts about the future. Make your responses very specific, for example:

*My doctor said that my blood pressure is too high.*
*Rumors about downsizing are upsetting me—and they're making my spouse nervous.*
*My son is having trouble at school.*
*I don't have time to do all I need to do.*
*My retirement fund just went up in smoke.*
*I'm alone and I don't know who will take care of me when I get old.*
*I can't control my eating/drinking/spending/ procrastination.*

Write down your answers.

_____

_____

_____

Writing your problems down will help get them out of your head and into fresh air.

**Question #2:**
**At this precise moment in my life, what are my chief "cosmic" worries?**

Include everything that is outside your family and your work. Think about your neighborhood, your city, your country, the world. As you consider this larger universe, again be very specific. Jot down your responses.

_____

_____

If you wish, add more:

_____

_____

A friendly warning: As you do this, your agitation may appear to increase. Remember: this clarification process isn't creating the problems; it simply names them. Unidentified stressors have a way of sucking up tremendous amounts of energy. Whether you are conscious of them or not, background rumblings have a significant impact on your balance and your health.

As you identify the sources of your discomfort, you gain increased control over the background static. You put yourself in the driver's seat vis-à-vis the energy-suckers.

### dive in

WHAT DO *YOU* WANT from reading this book?

If you say,

"I want to feel better," or

"I want to be more balanced,"

that won't cut it.

Get real, get definite. Make your intentions specific, even if they seem small. For example,

I want to:

*Develop a routine for beginning my workday with positive energy.*
*Schedule three periods of "me time" during the week.*

*Decide on two specific ways to spend time with my family.*
*Find a calm way to deal with email.*
*Shake my habit of taking problems to bed with me.*

Write down two or three specific goals. If you target your goals clearly, you greatly improve your chances of achieving them.

_____

_____

Congratulations for performing these three steps. By taking the time to chill out, warm up, and dive in, you have already moved yourself towards healthier balance.

You are now prepped to learn the first strategy.

If it's possible, set aside one hour right now to dedicate to your own balance training. If you can't take a full hour now, know that you can learn the Strategies one at a time.

Take a chunk of time now to dive into the first Strategy.

chapter 4

# OASIS: 60-second strategies

"You can't stop the waves
            but you can learn to surf."[1]

TRY AS YOU MAY, YOU CAN'T STILL THE WORLD.
Twenty-five hundred years ago the Greek philos-
opher Heraclitus summed it up:

"There is nothing permanent except change."[2]

Heraclitus lived in the Mediterranean, so he saw
lots of waves. Like Jon Kabat-Zinn, the originator of
the Mindfulness-Based Stress Reduction Clinic at
the University of Massachusetts, he probably found
a variety of useful ways to ride the waves.

The OASIS Strategies will help you navigate even
the difficult changes in your life with more skill. You
can learn to ride your personal and cosmic crises
with more control, more ease.

As you use the four Strategies, you will strengthen
the four domains of your total health: physical,
intellectual, emotional, and spiritual.

Here are the four key Strategies:

> **4-D**
> **3-B-C**
> **Cue-2-Do**
> **1 Stone**

You will need about fifteen minutes to learn each Strategy. Scan this chapter to get an overview of all the Strategies. If you're eager to experiment with each Strategy immediately, you may decide to read only the "goals," "how to do," and "benefits" for each Strategy. You may return later to know more about "who does? when? why" and "background."

After you've scanned the chapter, come back ready to experiment with the first Strategy.

Note well: research shows that usually we remember only

10% of what we read,

26% of what we hear,

30% of what we see, and

50% of what we see and hear

On the other hand, we remember 90% of what we say while doing a related activity.[3] Who can argue with that?

Prepare yourself to *do* the first Strategy. And go ahead. Say it out loud as you do it. What do you have to lose?

# 4-D = Four-Directions

## stretch your body

**goals**

- Give your body a break.
- Rinse off your mind.

4-D is a treat for your total self. By consciously engaging breath and body, you immediately
- relax tense muscles
- clear mental clutter
- gain a larger view of your immediate situation
- reset your emotions.

## how to do the 4-D

MAKE SURE THAT YOU HAVE AT LEAST FIFTEEN UNINTERRUPTED MINUTES right now. Find a private, comfortable space. The location doesn't need to be fancy, just a place where you can stretch out mentally and physically without being disturbed.

Commit to this time for yourself. Make sure that you mean it. When you take yourself seriously, others will be more likely to do the same.

- Turn off your cellphone.
- Let your voicemail take care of your other phone.
- If co-workers, kids or apartment-mates are around, let them know that you need private time.
- Hang a "Do Not Disturb" sign on your door.
- Loosen your belt or anything else that may constrict your breathing.
- If you like, take your shoes off.

Read over the instructions for Four-Directions. Then put your book where you can glance at it. Now:

- Stand.
- Exhale deeply. Loosen your lips as you release the breath. As much as possible, let your worries sail out with the exhale.
- Inhale gently through your nose. Keep this easy out-in rhythm going as you begin to pay attention to the rest of your body.
- Make space for your spine and head to lengthen up easily towards the ceiling. Picture pockets of easy space between each of your vertebrae.
- Let your arms hang down loosely. Your hands and fingers are unclenched, easy.
- Let your entire weight go to gravity. You don't need to carry a thing. Let the earth give you support. Let gravity do its job.

Now that you are firmly planted, you are ready to do the actual 4-D.

1. Stretch your arms and entire body to the ceiling, to the sky, as you say the word "*North!*" out loud in a full voice. . . . Really feel the stretch. . . . Now exhale. . . . Let your worries go out on a long exhale. . . .

Now let a new breath in . . . lots of room for it. . . . Keep on stretching, reaching. . . . Now let that stretch ease off.

2. Bend at your waist. . . . Let your head and whole upper torso drop towards the floor, the earth, as you say the word *"South!"* Go as far down as your body allows. . . . It's okay to bend your knees slightly. . . . Easy does it. . . . Let your heavy head simply hang. . . . Exhale. . . . Very gradually come back to standing, inhaling as you do.

3. Stretch out both arms in front of you. Extend your fingers as far as they can reach. Wiggle them. Then swing your arms and fingers, along with your whole torso, to the east. Say the word *"East!"* . . . Let the sound ring out as you stretch eastward. How far can your arms reach? How far on the horizon can you see? Let the view come into your eyes. If you see clutter, simply let it go on the exhale. Come back to center with your arms still extended in front of you.

4. Now swing your arms, along with your whole upper torso, to the west. Announce

> that direction *"West!"* as if you're really
> reaching out to the West Coast . . . and
> then to the ocean and sky beyond the coast
> . . . Stretch with your shoulders . . . your
> arms . . . your entire torso, clear down to
> your feet. . . . Enjoy your body's ability to
> experience the world from different
> vantage points. Come back to center. Feel
> your feet solidly on the ground.

That's it. Take another breath or two to enjoy yourself.

When you are finished, remove your "Do Not Disturb" sign. You're ready to go back into business—with whatever attitude you choose.

### benefits of 4-D

SIMPLE, NO? TOO SIMPLE to make a difference?

Do it.

You'll be amazed at how this sixty-second tool will increase your effectiveness—and your sanity. Stretching your body with clear intention can redirect your physiology, your fatigue level, and your emotional outlook.

Studies indicate that exercise, even an activity as basic as 4-D can:

- improve mood
- enhance blood flow and cardiovascular fitness
- improve memory
- increase bone density
- improve sleep
- reduce stress
- enhance self-image
- make energy utilization more efficient
- increase muscle tone and relaxation
- diminish biological markers of aging.[4]

Not bad for a no-charge one-minute stretch.

### who uses 4-D? when? why?

BRIAN, AN ARCHITECT:

"I often get sucked up in computer glaze and I lose focus. Now I set my watch to beep on the hour to remind me to take a 4-D break. I stand up, do it, then go back to my screen to design. It clears my head."

Yolanda manages a fifteen-person staff.

"I often begin my meetings with a standing 4-D to wake us up. It moves us out of whatever rut we were in. Sometimes, when other people lead the 4-D, they add their personal touches. Laura likes to travel; instead of saying 'North, South, East, West,' she'll take us to 'Alaska, Patagonia, Paris, Hawaii.' Larry prefers to do the 4-D with food: 'pizza, sub sandwich, grapefruit, spaghetti.' Doesn't seem to matter which words we use, the stretch and the words help us think with a larger perspective."

Tom is more reserved. After an especially difficult phone call with a client,

"I close my office door, look out the window and do a 4-D. Shakes off that last phone call and preps me for what's next."

Maria lives in a third-floor walk-up apartment with her aging mother and two young daughters.

"I don't have time or money to go to the gym and I'm always tired, so I had to figure out something for exercise. I finally got it! I have to carry my laundry baskets down to the basement. I used to hate this task and always felt crummy when I did it. I decided to shift my attitude to see if it would make a difference. It did."

Now, before carrying the dirty laundry down, Maria does a full-stretch 4-D. Then she takes a deep breath, expands her consciousness, and tells her body that she's about to give it a delicious workout.

> "I open my apartment door, pick up the basket and very deliberately feel each step under my feet as I go down the three flights."

Maria says that doing laundry is still a chore but she's less resentful now and more refreshed. While she's waiting for the loads to dry, she rewards herself with a walk in the fresh air outside.

> "If the weather's bad, I read a book for pleasure. And I stand up to stretch between the chapters."

## 4-D variations

AT A BORING CONFERENCE or in a situation that's getting you riled up? You might be thinking,

> "I'd sure like to shift this situation. But there's no way I can stand up and do a 4-D here. . . ."

You have alternatives.

Marianne:

> "Sometimes our board meetings drag on longer than I'd like. So I stretch out my legs under the table and do a *Foot 4-D*. I really extend south . . . east . . . west . . . and I remember to breathe. It gives me fresh energy, and nobody even notices I'm doing it."

Jeff does a brief *Hand 4-D*, also under the table, before settling on the details of a contract with tough clients:

> "I flex my wrists, hands, fingers, really extending them as far as I can in each direction. Loosens me up. Helps me notice details I may have missed."

4-D is a use-it-anywhere tool. Customize it to your needs and your mood. If you're in a situation where you really can't move, do a *Visual 4-D*. Let your eyes do a north-south-east-west scan to take in the larger picture.

About the only time not to use 4-D is when you're driving. But then again, if you're stuck in traffic or waiting for a light to change, you can always do a *Head-and-Shoulders 4-D*.

Do a *Standing 4-D* on your own right now. Anchor it in.

Decide on two specific times today when you will practice 4-D again.

Mark the times on your schedule, or set your watch to remind you.

Take an easy breath.

Now you're ready for the next strategy.

Decide whether you want to do it now or if you'd rather take a break first.

Your choice.

Do what works best for you.

# 3-B-C = Three-Breath-Countdown

## calm your mind

**goals**

- Stop the whirl.
- Drop the turmoil.
- Move from craziness to calm.

"YOU WESTERNERS. YOU'RE SO ONE-DIMENSIONAL. You don't even know how to breathe!"

So said Lous, my Indonesian mentor, when I whined about a grueling day at my job in Barcelona.

Breath is our most basic survival tool. Ironically, it's often the first thing to go when things get crazy. Lous knew that was true about me, so she sat me down that afternoon and initiated me into Real Breathing 101. I pass on her teaching to you. The basic instructions are hers; the variations are mine.

I offer you three breathing strategies that can give you instant calm: the *Emergency 3-B-C* and two forms of *Preventive 3-B-C*.

## how to do the *emergency 3-B-C*

- REST BOTH HANDS ON YOUR BELLY. . . . Bring your attention to your breath. . . . Send it out. . . . Let your lips be soft. . . . Purse them open a tiny bit to let the air come out. . . . Very gradually, let all the breath out. . . . Your worries can exit with your exhale. . . . Hear your breath going out. . . . Let your hands feel your belly go in. This is the long exhale.
- Now you're ready for the inhale.

- Keep your hands on your belly. . . . Close your lips gently. Let the air come in through your nostrils . . . softly . . . gently . . . no need to pull it in. . . . Nature abhors a vacuum, so your belly will fill up on its own. . . . Just allow room for the air to come in . . . easily. . . . Let it come all the way down. . . . Feel it pushing your hands out as your belly expands. That's the full inhale. You've got it. Just keep it going.
- Breathe out and in two more times, slowly, deliberately. . . . Take time to reach easy emptiness on the exhale and spacious fullness on the inhale. Let the breath do its thing. It's been doing it for centuries. Your body is simply one of its latest vehicles.

That's it.
Ask yourself:

"What is different in my body and in my mind from one minute ago?"

Notice any shifts with curiosity rather than with judgment.

## how to do the *preventive 3-B-C*

BEGIN WITH AN INHALE rather than an exhale.

Why? In the *Preventive 3-B-C*, you want your initial inhale to bring in calmness immediately, whereas in an emergency your initial exhale can dispel extreme emotions that may throw you off balance.

To practice the *Preventive 3-B-C*, try the two forms below.

### here-and-now *preventive 3-B-C*

- RIGHT NOW, TAKE A MINUTE TO LOOK AROUND YOU, wherever you are. It doesn't matter if you're inside or outside, whether you're in a "beautiful" place or an ordinary place.

- Let your eyes take in the colors, the objects around you.

- Find one object or one color that—for whatever reason—appeals to you.

- Let your hands rest on your belly. Then, as you inhale softly and deeply, focus on this color or object. Invite the color, the texture, and the form to come into you.

- As you inhale and exhale three times, invite the beauty, the "rightness" of the appeal, to come into your breath and into your being.

■ When you have finished the three breaths, take a little time to absorb what has just happened. You may notice that your heart rate has slowed, that you feel calmer than before, that your mind is less busy. Give yourself time to appreciate this. Allow your physiology time to integrate this window of spacious calmness.

## mini-vacation *preventive 3-B-C*: Personal Palm Pilot

SOMETIMES YOU NEED A BREAK. Maybe the room you're in really is ugly, or it's too hectic: wherever you look, there are reminders of projects you need to finish, things that need to be put away or dealt with, phone calls to return, emails begging for an answer. Instead of hanging out in this *Here-and-Now*, you can make a conscious choice to go to a more refreshing *There-and-Then*.

Give yourself a mini-vacation. No need to call a travel agent. Just turn away from your computer or desk. Put your phone on answer mode and turn the ring volume down. Sit comfortably in your chair or stretch out on the floor. Get ready to do my version of the Personal Palm Pilot:

- Close your eyes gently. Let your mind wander off to any place it wants to go—a favorite vacation place you have been to or a place that you dream of visiting. The only criteria are that it be beautiful and that it be restful for you. Allow several possibilities to float in front of you. See the colors, feel the temperature, the textures. Then decide on one place, and one very specific spot in that place. Name the spot. Then go there. See what time of day or night it is.

- Put your palms together. Rub them against each other until you feel their warmth. Then gently place your palms over your closed eyes. Bring up the picture of your vacation place. As you focus on this place of beauty, of rest, take a deliciously long inhale. Feel the temperature, the wind. See the colors—all of them. Touch the textures. Invite the sounds to wash over you.

- As you exhale, let your body sink into relaxation. Let your mind delight in the ease. . . .

- Inhale and exhale three times, softly, fully. Enjoy your vacation.

When you have finished your three breaths, take a little time to savor your trip. Know that you can be your own Palm Pilot and go there any time you wish. It won't cost you a cent.

Draw a little sketch or write a few words that capture the essence of that place for you. You may want to copy this on to colored paper. Post it where you can see it.

My mini-vacation place

_____

What I like about it

_____

_____

How I feel when I'm there

_____

_____

## benefits of 3-B-C

THE 3-B-C GIVES YOUR BRAIN AND YOUR BODY access to the "food" they need to do their jobs efficiently. Instead of being at the mercy of your individual knee-jerk reactions, you can train yourself to respond to events with increased clarity. You can learn how to calm yourself. Gestalt therapist Fritz Perls noted, "Fear is excitement without breath." I would add that panic is often fear—whether rational or irrational—without breath.

When you use the *Emergency 3-B-C*, you give yourself the chance to blow off steam without hurting anyone, including yourself. By beginning with an exhale in emergencies, you dissipate the unbalance caused by fear, anger or anxiety. The pause allows you to notice with more clarity what is actually happening and to choose how you want to respond.

If you don't have time to take three breaths, stop and take one. This split-second *stop* can often mean the difference between disaster and deliverance for your own emotional and physical health as well as for your relations with the people around you.

When you practice either form of the *Preventive 3-B-C* in non-emergencies, you build your "emotional muscles." Then, when something whacks you unexpectedly, you'll be more able to respond with a clearer mind and a calmer heart. If you have those muscles tuned, your ability to act wisely will be much more likely to kick in.

Whether you do the *Here-and-Now 3-B-C* or take the mini-vacation, know that you are giving your heart, your body, and your mind a treat. In the space of sixty seconds, and without spending a penny, you can lower your blood pressure, air out your mental baggage, and reduce your emotional dis-ease.

## how this strategy got its name

ON A JANUARY AFTERNOON, my colleague Bonnie phoned me.

> "Millie, our fifth-graders are having a lot of trouble with bullying and impulse control. Can you come in and teach them something that might help?"

I went to Bonnie's classroom the following week. Fifteen boys and girls made a list of things that put them on edge:

- *When somebody calls me names.*
- *When a kid picks on me and I don't know what to do about it.*
- *When something sad is happening. Like my mom is really sick and I'm afraid, but I don't know what to do.*

- *When I don't know something I think I should know, and I feel stupid, and I feel like everybody is looking at me.*
- *When I get mad and want to hit somebody or do something, and I know I'll get in more trouble if I do.*

I asked the kids, "Would you like to learn some tools that might help you when you're feeling pressured?" They were eager and ready.

I taught them the 4-D stretch. They got it. Then I showed them how to slow down and take three breaths whenever they needed to chill out: maybe when the teacher said something tough to them, when another kid was mean, or when they felt like hitting somebody. I didn't give the technique a name but just taught them how to put their hands on their bellies—being fifth graders, they snickered at that word—and pay attention to their breath.

When I visited a week later, I asked the group, "How did it go?" Gary, who hadn't said a word the week before, shot his hand up and said, "I did it! I did it!—the 3-B-C! It really worked!"

Since I couldn't remember anything about 3-B-C, I had no idea what Gary was talking about. I asked, "What do you mean?" Gary eagerly told his story:

"I was in gym class. I hate gym class because nobody ever picks me. I was sitting on the bench and, like always, nobody chose me. I was afraid I was going to cry. And I HATE to cry in front of everybody. So all of a sudden I remembered the 3-B-C. You know—that Three-Breath-Countdown that we did last week. So I did it. I put my hands on my stomach; I concentrated real hard the way you said. I let all that bad stuff go out on the first breath, and then I took in three good breaths. And you know what? It worked. I didn't cry—and somebody chose me!"

## who uses 3-B-C? when? why?

KIDS AREN'T THE ONLY ONES who have to deal with things going wrong and with people looking at them disapprovingly. My adult clients tell me how upset they become when they receive a poor evaluation at work, when there is discord in their relationships, when the stock market plunges, when world crises impinge on their sense of safety, or when the commute home is hellish.

Many clients report that they have begun to use the Three-Breath-Countdown strategy almost any time, any place. It's a quick, efficient way to jump out of the overwhelm into balance. Patti reports that if she's too rushed to do a 3-B-C, she simply does a 1-B-C, starting with one long exhale and finishing with a full inhale.

## in non-stress situations: use the *preventive 3-B-C*

DEBBIE KEEPS A PHOTO of her favorite vacation place on her desk:

> "I take a mini-vacation at least once a day, usually right after lunch. If I'm really stressed, I take more than one."

Carly does a conscious 3-B-C as an exit-entrance ritual:

> "I do it before I leave home in the morning and then again when I leave my office. It helps me not carry extra mental stuff with me as I go from one place to the other."

Tim:

> "I take three breaths before I make a difficult phone call. And if I'm involved in a project, I decide whether or not to answer a call. If I do pick up, I take a 1-B-C to put myself into a focused frame before answering."

Susan is trying to lose weight:

> "I used to gobble food without tasting it. Now, before I eat, I do a 3-B-C. It helps me notice whether I'm really hungry for food or if I want something else."

She then chooses accordingly. When she is ready to eat, she pauses again.

> "This brief 'pay-attention-to-now' helps me slow down before I pick up my fork. I actually see what I'm eating now and I enjoy the flavors more."

Tony had a hard time getting a good night's sleep:

> "I used to end the day by watching the late-night news. Thought I needed to do it to be up on things. Well, I was up, all right, for most of the night. I made a radical—for me—switch. Now, instead of TV, I end the day with a 3-B-C. I take time to ask, 'What three things happened today that I feel good about?' Then I give the answers some breathing space. I'm sleeping much better. I can always catch the news in the morning."

*Preventive 3-B-Cs* are pleasurable workouts. They strengthen your emotional muscles to be able to respond with calmness rather than to react with impulsiveness.

## in tough situations: use the *emergency 3-B-C*

WHETHER AN UPSET IS BIG OR SMALL, you can always profit from a 3-B-C. Use the *Emergency 3-B-C* when:

- someone attacks you verbally
- you get a bad review at work
- you receive devastating news about a family member
- somebody cuts you off in traffic
- a news flash hits you in the gut

Alan, co-owner of a manufacturing firm, complained that he never had any time for himself. He routinely took his work pressures with him when he left his office for the forty-five-minute drive home. He explained further:

"I usually turn on the radio when I hit I-95. I listen to news commentators all the way home to give me a break and to take my mind off all the crazy drivers. Those drivers really *are* crazy; they make me so angry. When I get home, I'm exhausted and I really need time just for me. I don't want to talk to anybody or deal with anything. My wife and kids aren't especially wild about this routine of mine."

Alan was a prime candidate for a quick fix, so I taught him the 3-B-C.

It wasn't easy for Alan to clear out space in his schedule, even for a one-minute activity. It was even more challenging for him to clear out space in his head. When Alan did begin to take a brief snatch of time to breathe, he was able to "look at myself from a distance," as he put it. From this viewpoint, he realized that he could switch to an entirely different way of transitioning from work to home:

> "Here's what I do now: I schedule in ten minutes for myself before I leave my office. I call it my ten-minute putt time. Instead of trying to make one more phone call, I take time for me. I do a 3-B-C, and then I put everything in order so that I can leave it here and pick it up again when I'm back tomorrow. Then, when I get in my car, no more news. I've got some favorite CDs now, including Bruce Springsteen and Cheryl Crow. They relax me, make me feel good. That feels like time for me. If a guy cuts in front of me and I feel myself getting steamed up, I do another 3-B-C.

> "Now when I get home, I don't have to hide out to get time for myself; I've already had it. I actually talk to my wife now. And even my kids look forward to me walking in the door."

Stopping for a 3-B-C has consequences much larger than are apparent in that moment. *Emergency* and *Preventive 3-B-Cs* are streamlined ways to control your physical and emotional reactions, broker your own energy, and take better care of your health. As a bonus, you stand a good chance of improving your relationships with the people around you— whether on the highway, at work, or at home.

To practice this strategy right now, look ahead to a situation that you expect to be challenging for you.

Picture it in as much detail as possible.

Then see yourself doing a 3-B-C.

# Cue-2-Do

## change your brain

**goals**

- Use your aches and pains as cues.
- Change channels from discomfort to pleasure.

FEEL A HEADACHE COMING ON? Notice tightness in your shoulders?

"Stress and pain don't disappear. Indeed, they only intensify their demand for attention, shouting at us until we notice."[5]

We all have our special aches and pains. The Cue-2-Do Strategy teaches you to utilize your everyday physical and emotional discomforts as cues. When you learn to recognize your signals, you can take advantage of them to help you move away from pain and towards health.

To use this strategy, you need to recognize your particular cues, your unique distress signals. You also need to become aware of what emotion or emotions might be connected to those cues at a particular time. If you're like most people, you have a wide range of reactions to any particular situation. I call these reactions your *emotional channels*.

Once you identify your personal cues, you're ready to respond to these five key questions.

1. What is your cue right now?
2. What is that cue signaling? What channel are you on?
3. What's the current drama on that channel?
4. Is there anything you can do and want to do right now about the situation?
5. What action is best for you right now?

## how to do the Cue-2-Do

HAVE PEN AND PAPER HANDY. Right now, see if you can determine:

What are *your* distress signals? Precisely where do you notice them? Head? Stomach? Throat? Chest? Hands? Mind? Heart?

_____

_____

*What specifically do you notice* about each? Dull throbbing in your left temple? Cold sweat in your palms? I mean the *where* and *what* quite literally. Locate exactly where in your body or in your mind you become aware of discomfort. Find the words that best describe the feeling in that place. Write down your answers in detail.

_____

_____

When you pay very close attention to yourself, you will probably notice that you have different cues for different situations. Here's what some of my clients report.

Bruce:

"When I'm angry, I feel a pounding across the front of my forehead and tightness in my fists."

Mary Ann:

"If somebody says something that hurts me, my stomach gets queasy, my throat tightens, and my mind starts to blur."

Amanda:

"My breathing gets shallow and my heart races when something frightens me."

---

### the five Cue-2-Do questions

ONCE YOU ISOLATE YOUR PERSONAL SIGNALS, you're ready for Cue-2-Do's five questions. Your honest responses will help you understand your discomfort and point you to your most useful response.

1. What is *my cue* right now? Precisely where am I feeling it? Exactly what does it feel like?

   _____

   _____

---

2. What is that cue signaling? What *emotional channel* am I on? Anger? Worry? Frustration? Depression? Anxiety? Several channels at once?

_____

_____

3. What's the *current drama* on that channel? Is it a rerun of a past event, a real-life situation right now that needs my immediate attention, or an uneasy fear of something that might happen if. . .?

_____

_____

4. Is there anything *I can do* and *want to do right now* about the situation?

_____

_____

5. *What action* is best for me right now?

_____

_____

If your answer to #4 is yes, then *take the appropriate action* immediately.

If it's no, *change channels*. Ask yourself: "What emotion do I want to let go of? What emotion do I want to invite in to replace it?" Then switch channels immediately.

To make this strategy work for you, stop reading right now.

- Perform a thorough body/mind check.
- Notice if you are aware of any discomfort.
- If you identify something, go through the five questions and see what you come up with.

When you are clear, take action.

## benefits of Cue-2-Do

MOST OF US HAVE WHAT I CALL *default modes*. One of my major default modes is worry. When I slip into the worry groove, I trigger physiological reactions that have far-reaching effects on my well-being: the worry channel immediately clouds my mind, dampens my spirit, makes me fearful and upsets my immune system.

What is *your* primary default mode? Anger? Fear? Sadness? Impatience? If you have *happy* as a default mode, count yourself fortunate, especially if it's not the Pollyanna type of happiness. When you slip into a default emotion, whether it be an upper or a downer, you can be certain that it has consequences in all four of your health domains: physical, intellectual, emotional and spiritual.

If you are able to identify your cues and know what they signify, you have a better chance of knowing what *emotional channel* you are on. And you can begin to detect whether the drama is about the actual current situation or if it's tapping into an old soap opera. Once you are clear about that, you can make decisions that are both appropriate and effective. When you are not clear about what is really going on and when you can't interpret your mixture of feelings about the situation, your chances of taking the best action are substantially impaired.

The research of psychologists Peter Salovey and Daniel Goleman helps us to have an increased appreciation of our emotional intelligence. Their work provides evidence that we humans have a unique ability to shape our own lives and, in so doing, to have significant impact on ourselves and on the people and environment around us.

When you practice the Cue-2-Do Strategy, you utilize your emotional intelligence to counteract the power of what Goleman calls "destructive emotions."[6] By consciously refocusing, by opting to move towards a more beneficial emotion, you forge the beginning of a new neural pathway. By your minute-to-minute conscious choices, you actually change the wiring of your brain.

### who uses Cue-2-Do? when? why?

LINDA LOVES HER JOB at a major corporation but her responsibilities often intrude on her outside life.

> "I manage various groups of people who have multiple duties. Whenever there's a problem, I'm the one who needs to fix it."

Last week, a few minutes before she was leaving for the day, Linda's phone rang. She picked it up. Another problem.

> "I felt my stomach tighten immediately. I paused and thought, 'Aha! That's my cue!' It hit me: 'I'm on my desperation-won't-get-any-sleep-tonight channel.' Once I spotted that, I asked myself, 'Is there anything I *can* do and *want* to do about the situation right now?' That question helped me realize that I needed more information before I could act. Since I couldn't get that info until the morning, I decided that my best option was to switch channels.

> "Usually I would have taken the problem home with me, stewed about it and had a sleepless

night. As soon as I switched from the sleepless-night channel to the have-a-good-night's-sleep channel, I felt much better."

John has run his family business for three decades and is looking forward to retirement. A few months ago he began experiencing unusual physical pain. He was concerned because heart disease runs in his family. John's doctor advised him to learn how to reduce his stress, so he came to me. I taught John the OASIS Strategies and he began using them. As he worked the Cue-2-Do Strategy, John realized that his major default mode was fear. Two weeks after he began his work with me, John received alarming financial news about his company.

> "I immediately felt my heart constrict. But in that precise moment I plugged in to Cue-2-Do to switch from fear to the easy-does-it channel. It took the pressure off right away. Then, later, I was able to deal with things with less anxiety."

Chuck emailed me to say:

> "I put some techniques into practice when I was flying home from a workshop. I was in two traffic jams on the way to the airport, missed a turn, and then left my cellphone in the rental car. On the flight, I focused on one good thing and went from poor-me into problem-solving mode,

which I can do well. They found the phone and they are sending it to me today."

Jane took two days off from teaching to finish writing an article. Every time she began working at her laptop, a sharp pain in her abdomen distracted her.

"I asked myself the Cue-2-Do questions and recognized that the pain was triggering fear. I've had this pain off and on for weeks but had been doing my best to ignore it. When I realized how persistent the pain was, I asked myself, 'Is there anything I can and want to do about it right now?' I knew that I really needed to stay and finish the article but I decided to stop right then and call my doctor's office to set up an appointment. It felt good to take definite action. After the call I was able to focus on the article more easily. And, funny thing, the pain seemed to subside."

Stella was in the High Sierras for a two-week trek with friends. When she noticed billows of smoke from a forest fire slightly to the south of their camp, her immediate reaction was panic.

"I felt my mind start to go berserk and I realized I was on the deer-in-the-headlights channel. I made a deliberate choice to get off that channel. I chose to go to calmness, and that immediately reminded me of my boyfriend Chris. He's always so calm. He's an experienced climber and teaches wilderness safety. Thinking of Chris shifted my energy. I became calm enough to make the right decisions for my safety."

## how i "discovered" Cue-2-Do

AS I DROVE TO MEET MY FRIEND GENE FOR LUNCH, I heard the local news:

"Another teenager was shot last night near Hillhouse High School. The seventeen-year-old boy is in critical condition at St. Raphael's Hospital. This is the third shooting of a teenager in the last two weeks. One young man has died; two remain in guarded condition."

I felt my stomach tighten and sensed the familiar tingling of a migraine headache beginning above my left eye. Our sons are teenagers, and we live two blocks from that high school.

When I caught up with Gene, I told him how upset I was, how my stomach and head ached, and how that always occurred whenever something bad happened. I added, somewhat petulantly,

"It's not fair. Bad news doesn't seem to bother other people that much. But my body goes crazy and I can't do anything about it. I got that trait from my mother and she got it from her mother. It's genetic."

Gene said, rather nonchalantly,

"Aw, Millie, that's not genetic. That's just a habit."

Gene had no idea that in that instant his words initiated a major change in my behavior. I thought:

"If what he says is true, I'm not trapped. I have a choice: I can let this depressive ruminating dig deeper into me or I can shift my focus to something else."

As Gene and I continued to walk down Trumbull Street towards Clark's Dairy, I devised an experiment: Could I switch from my well-oiled *worry* channel to a *find-one-thing-that's-okay-in-my-life* channel? I looked up and saw that the sun was still in the sky. That was one thing that was okay, even though someone's young son had been shot last night. I could feel that the simple act of changing my focus from *worry* to *okay* was relieving the swirling in my stomach and the pain of my migraine.

I experimented with *changing channels* several times later that day and throughout the rest of the week. As I played with the experiment, I noticed that when I paid close attention to my pain, it would often give me clues about what I was feeling emotionally. A churning stomach often meant that I was worried or afraid. A beginning migraine often indicated that I felt out of control, sad, or angry.

I began to realize that my physical pains weren't something to be avoided or denied: I could use them as powerful cues. Instead of dragging me down, they could be invitations for me to notice what was going on and to do something about it.

This shouldn't have surprised me. My years of training with body/mind pioneer Ilana Rubenfeld had impressed on me the certainty of the body's wisdom. Rubenfeld appreciates the intricate interrelationship between our minds and our bodies. She knows that when we ignore the body's signals, we invite more trouble for ourselves.

John's quick action, when he felt his heart constrict, helped him begin to reset his *bad news* habit. He is shifting from an old groove to a new pattern that allows space for both his heart and his mind to work with less pressure.

Linda, Chuck, Jane and Stella also used their body's cues to work with their emotions. When they did this, they made changes in their physiology and in their mood. And, in doing this, they and John were rewiring their brains to tip themselves back to better balance.

To practice Cue-2-Do now, think of a recent time when you know that you slipped into a non-productive default mode. Revisit the incident. Identify your signals in any or all of the four domains: physical, intellectual, emotional, spiritual. Then ask yourself the five questions:

1.  What is my cue right now?

    _____

2.  What is that cue signaling? What channel am I on?

    _____

3.  What's the current drama on that channel?

    _____

4.  Is there anything I can do and want to do right now about the situation?

    _____

5.  What action is best for me right now?

    _____

    _____

For extra practice, look ahead to an upcoming event. Target a situation that you know from past experience has the potential to knock you off balance. Strategize your behavior by performing a *Future Cue-2-Do*.

- Look at your picture clearly.
- Be sure to include the cast of characters.
- See yourself and your usual responses to that type of situation.
- Make a choice about how you want to respond: in your usual way or differently?
- See yourself now making the choice and acting on it.

Take a minute now to write down what you learned from this *Future Cue-2-Do* experiment. Choose a *cue word* or *cue symbol* to help you remember how you want to respond in that coming situation.

What I learned:_____

_____

_____

My cue word/symbol:

_____

# 1 Stone

## balance your total self

"You can observe a lot by watching."[7]

Yogi Berra

**goals**

- Open your eyes.
- Gather your wits.
- See the big picture.

1 STONE IS THE SIMPLEST, and perhaps the most important, of the OASIS Strategies. It's the ultimate *rinse cycle*. 1 Stone can give you an immediate oasis, wherever you may be.

## how to do 1 Stone

- PLACE A STONE, or any object of comfort, in the palm of your hand.
- With relaxed attention, look at the stone. Notice the variations in its color, its texture, its grain.
- Feel the stone in your hand. How heavy does it feel? Is it cool or warm?
- With your eyes open, breathe in and out very slowly as you look at the stone.
- Take nine more in-and-out breaths as you continue looking at the stone. If your mind wanders somewhere else, that's okay. That's what minds do. Just bring it back gently to the stone and your breath.

When you finish the ten breaths, stay with your stone a bit longer. What do you notice now about your body? Your breathing? Your heartbeat? Your thoughts?

Gradually let your eyes move from the stone to your surroundings. Keep on breathing as you let the larger picture come into your consciousness.

Take this easy awareness with you as you make the transition into the next moment of your day.

## benefits of 1 Stone

CENTURIES OF TRADITION in both the East and the West bear witness to the spiritual value of meditation.

More recent medical studies by Dr. Herbert Benson and others verify its health benefits.[8] Accounts in medical newsletters and sports magazines frequently refer to the psychological and emotional power of meditation. As of the 1990s, imaging techniques provide concrete evidence of the physiological changes that occur in the brain, mind, and body as a result of the extensive practice of meditation.

In my work with clients, I find that many are dismissive of or intimidated by the notion of meditation; they think it's either "too new-agey" or "for spiritual people only." Those who do try it often believe that the purpose of meditating is to block out things from their minds, and they close their eyes to be able to do this. This type of meditation often gives them some reprieve. However, they complain that, in the long run, it doesn't really help. Being a good escape artist is sometimes useful but retreating and/or avoiding is not always the best choice.

The ability to *stay focused*, to be present, in challenging circumstances is an entirely different skill. I know of no other method that is as effective as the 1 Stone ten-breath meditation, with eyes open.

What is unique about the *1 Stone* meditation is that it is:

- **extremely simple**
- **tangible**: the physical connection with a stone or other object cuts through resistance and distraction
- **done with eyes open**: this brings you to the here-and-now reality
- **appealing**: CEOs, athletes, five-year-olds, ninety-five-year olds, parents, accountants, politicians, prison inmates, clergy, and therapists pick it up quickly and use it frequently
- **immediately effective**: within less than a minute, practitioners report feeling calmer and clearer

### how i learned the 1 Stone strategy

THE SUMMER FOLLOWING MY BIKE ACCIDENT, the left side of my face was still numb and my mind was not moving as agilely as it had before my head hit the pavement. My husband suggested that a quiet week in the country might be good medicine. My neighbor Lynn told me about a retreat at Omega Institute, in rural New York, in July. I wasn't sure I would be able to do long stretches of sitting at attention with a Buddhist monk, but I decided to give it a shot.

It rained almost all week. I sat with the group when it felt okay and I lay down when my body needed to rest. When the sun finally broke out on the fourth day, the retreat leader Thich Nhat Hanh, a Vietnamese monk who had been nominated for the Nobel Peace Prize, invited the children in the group to walk down to the lake with him. We adults followed.

When we reached the lake's edge, the tiny monk stooped down to pick up a stone and invited the children to do the same. He asked the children to place the stone in their hands and he would teach them the ten-breath meditation. He gathered the children with his eyes and said,

"Look at your stone. Notice its color, its shape. Feel it in your hand. Now we're going to take ten easy breaths, in and out, looking at the stone.

Don't worry about what your mind does. It may run off to lots of other places. That's what our minds do. When you notice it running, don't fuss at it. Just come back to your stone, look at it and go to your next breath."

The entire lake area became noticeably quieter as the children breathed with their stones. After the ten breaths, the monk gave the kids a few minutes to hang out with whatever it was that they had noticed. Then he gave them time to talk and ask questions. He knew that we adults were watching closely.

A scruffy ten-year-old boy asked, "Are you always so calm?" Nhat Hanh explained to the children and to us that it wasn't always easy for him to stay peaceful. He said that it was fairly easy for him to feel calm in his monastery. But when he went into the city to help the orphaned and wounded during the war in Vietnam, the needs were so intense that he lost his peacefulness. He went to the city several times but had to leave each time because he wasn't strong enough to deal with all the suffering. He realized that he needed to find a way to *be present* rather than retreat, no matter what was going on. He found that *breathing with the stone*, with his eyes *open*, was an immense help. This was a practice he could put in his pocket and carry into the city with him.

Little did I realize, as I watched this slightly-built monk instruct the children, that the simple breathing practice he taught them would be the very strategy that my client Nick would use ten years later to balance himself in his busy life.

### who uses 1 Stone? when? why?

"I'M A TYPE A, POSSIBLY AA, PERSONALITY, MILLIE, and I'm proud of it. I steer away from stress management pitches because I don't want to lose my drive. Besides, I don't have time for that kind of stuff."

Nick, 55-year-old CEO

Getting Nick to slow down, even for a minute, was a challenge. I first met him at the event celebrating his inauguration as CEO of a prestigious county-wide organization. After Nick's speech, his wife approached me:

"You've got to help him. Nick is so excited about this new position, but I'm really worried about him. He's already had two heart attacks and he just never stops. He's afraid if he slows down he'll lose his fire. He won't listen to me. Maybe he'll listen to you."

Somewhat to my surprise, Nick phoned two weeks later.

"Look, Millie, I don't really know what you do but I'm calling because my wife is pushing me."

I told Nick that I knew he had enough pressures in his life, and I certainly didn't want to pressure him into anything else. I assured him that I had no interest in dampening his fire. I said,

"Rather, I'd like to introduce you to a few quick strategies to help you balance your busy life. Who knows? They might hone your drive so that you can be even more effective—and stay healthy to boot."

Finally, perhaps because he was on a speakerphone and his wife was standing behind him, Nick agreed to come, but only for one visit. He came the following week, dove into the Strategies and grasped them quickly. In one hour Nick got what he needed. His favorite was 1 Stone.

### what if i don't have a stone?

IN A PINCH YOU CAN USE ANYTHING: a penny, a pencil, a paper-weight.

Why do I prefer a stone? Probably because that's how I first learned this exercise. But beyond that, stones evoke a sense of permanence, a connection with our origins and the larger universe, much more strongly than do objects of our day-to-day activities.

I like the smoothness and beauty of Japanese river stones. I usually find them at my local Pier 1 or at a garden store. You may have a favorite stone or shell from a special place. Use whatever works best for you.

Lynette keeps her stone on her desk at work.

> "I pick it up every once in a while, especially when I'm wrought up. It helps me gather my wits. I've been doing it for ten years. It still works."

Sally, a hospice nurse, keeps her stone in her car.

> "I go on home visits three days a week. That's my job: to be with the family as well as with the person who is dying. When the patient is about the same age as I am, and has kids as I do, it's especially tough. What I do now is: a few minutes before I reach the house, I find a quiet spot to pull over. I take out my stone and do my ten breaths. It helps me remember who I am, and what I'm here for. Then I can go in to meet the family more peacefully."

Marv, my bookkeeper, says,

"It's my sanity stone, especially during tax season. When I use the stone, I find it easier to tell a client he owes money."

Jim taught the stone meditation to his partner, who is diabetic. Jim said,

"Bob has trouble resisting sweet desserts. But when he's got his stone with him, it somehow reminds him to take it easy and pick something else."

One afternoon when her five-year-old son was pushing her near the end of her patience, Kim gave him a stone and did the ten-breath meditation with him. Recently Kim told me,

"Now, sometimes when I'm frantic, my son catches me: 'Mommy, you need to breathe.' We sit down and do it together."

THREE MONTHS AFTER MY ONE-HOUR SESSION with Nick, I ran into him downtown. He looked good in his trim business suit and, as usual, he was moving fast.

"Millie, great to see you!"

Nick took his hand out of his pocket to greet me. As we shook hands, I was surprised to feel a hard, warm object in his hand.

"Yep, it's the stone. I carry it with me all the time. Reminds me to take it easy."

You have now learned the four OASIS Strategies. You've had the chance to experiment with variations on each, and you've read about how various people are incorporating them into their daily lives.

You might want to use one of the Strategies now before you begin the next chapter.

Give yourself a break.

Choose your oasis.

chapter 5

# staying afloat in tough times

I try to take just
ONE DAY AT A TIME . . .

but lately several days
have attacked me at once

MY MOM HAD OCCASIONAL DAYS LIKE THIS years ago as she took care of us seven kids. But this feeling of "several days attacking me at once" comes around pretty often for most of us nowadays.

## bad news about stress

DO YOU KNOW THAT STRESS IN HUMANS

- contributes to 80% of major illnesses,
- is responsible for 75% to 90% of visits to doctors' offices, and
- costs businesses as much as $300 billion a year?[1]

Whether we like it or not, the following are facts of life in our time:

- stress is here to stay,
- stress factors are increasing exponentially in our personal lives and in the world, and
- our response to stress is the number one determinant of our personal health and happiness.

The *Women's Health Research at Yale Newsletter* verifies that depression and stress are risk factors for the development and progression of heart disease.[2] Recent evidence confirms that heart disease increases dramatically after stressful events. Researchers at St. Luke's-Roosevelt Hospital Center in New York City found that in the month following the 9/11 terrorist attacks in 2001, heart patients in the greater New York area suffered life-threatening heart arrhythmias at more than twice the usual rate.[3]

Not concerned about heart disease? You're still not free and clear. Hundreds of clinical studies cite stress as a factor in conditions such as:

- ✓ heightened anxiety
- ✓ fatigue
- ✓ depression
- ✓ inhibited memory function
- ✓ interrupted sleep
- ✓ lessened joy in life
- ✓ elevated blood pressure
- ✓ disturbed relationships
- ✓ lowered sexual functioning
- ✓ poor work performance
- ✓ impaired immune systems
- ✓ increased incidence of strokes and cancer.

How many of these might apply to you?

You probably don't need extensive documentation to point out the presence of personal stress. Your reaction while you're stuck in a traffic jam when you're already late for an appointment is proof enough. If, when you're at a standstill on the highway or on the train or in the airport, you hear news of targeted violence in the world or of random violence in your neighborhood, your stress level escalates.

A community counseling clinic in Georgia registered a six-fold increase in the number of people seeking help after terror alerts. "People are reporting headaches, insomnia, back pain, neck pain, disorientation," says Director Pierluigi Mancini. "But after a physical exam, we can't find a physical cause."[4] Add the uncertainty about the future of such heretofore staples as Social Security, Medicare, and established financial institutions, and you have a steady background of unpredictability and fear.

Research verifies that this on-guard state, along with the increased sense of helplessness that accompanies it, has a major impact on your physiology and your mental state.[5]

## causes of death: then and now

ACCORDING TO STATISTICS from the United States Department of Health and Human Services, the three leading causes of death in the USA in the early 1900s were pneumonia, tuberculosis and diarrhea/enteritis.

Contrast this with the three major killers in the first decade of the twenty-first century: heart disease, cancer, and stroke. If you add together the deaths from accidents, injuries, suicides, and assaults, you have the fourth leading cause of death in our times. In reference to these non-disease deaths, the numbers indicate that 85% of these occurrences are man-made, not "acts of God."[6]

These statistics highlight an interaction between human behavior and disease. Certainly, advances in twentieth-century and early twenty-first-century medicine have helped control the spread of deadly infectious and viral diseases. However, the leading four causes of death in this century have a clear relation to stress.

We may not *cause* cancer or heart disease, but how we choose to live has a definite impact both on our physical health and on our environment. And what we do to our environment in turn impacts our physical health.

## good news about stress

IF STRESS IS SO TERRIBLE, should we try to eliminate it? I don't think so. Programs that claim to erase stress from our lives miss the mark. As Dr. Hans Selye, the grandfather of stress physiology research, put it after decades of study: "Stress is the spice of life."[7]

Selye's conclusions affirm that stress:
- is a natural reaction,
- is neither negative nor positive, and
- is simply force applied to an object.

Your blood won't circulate unless your heart pushes it. Your knee doesn't bend unless you exert some force. Your brain conjures up new ideas when something stimulates it.

Clearly, the idea is not to get rid of stress. Rather it is to cultivate the right relationship with it. My husband, who has worked in construction and is a furniture designer, knows this:

"Sure, everything needs stress. It's an integral part of how structures hold together." He adds, "But of course, you wouldn't want to put an I-beam on an egg."

My Type A personality clients appreciate Selye's distinction between *eu-stress* (good stress) and *distress* (bad stress). They love quoting his statement:

"The only time that humans and animals are without stress is when they are dead."

The next time you notice that you are stressed, first of all be thankful that you are aware of it.

Then pause to ask, "What's this about?"

Then choose an OASIS Strategy to reset your balance to the best of your ability at that precise moment.

## great news: our brains are plastic

WHEN I STUDIED PSYCHOLOGY IN COLLEGE, my professors told me that I was near my prime and I had better take advantage of it because, before long, I'd start losing my brain cells.

They were wrong.

The hot word in brain research today is neuroplastic, a word my professors back then had never heard of. They'd be surprised to find articles about the brain's neuroplasticity in venues as varied as *Sports Illustrated, O: The Oprah Magazine*, and *Harvard Medical News*.

## couch potatoes and stockbrokers

WHY DO SOME PEOPLE RETAIN VIBRANCY while others fade? Issues of resiliency and quality of life have long intrigued Dr. Marian Diamond.

In one of her studies, Dr. Diamond experimented with two groups of rats. Group A, her *couch potato rats*, lived a rather sedentary and predictable life. In contrast, her Group B *stockbroker rats* had to deal with frequent changes in their routines; in addition, they faced various challenges to reach their food.

Diamond found that:

- the more sedentary rats, even if they were younger, developed senility factors more quickly than their stockbroker counter-parts,

- the active stockbroker rats demonstrated increased vitality and flexibility, and

- these changes were reflected both in their actions and in the anatomical structure of their brains: the stockbroker rats moved faster and their brains actually grew larger than the brains of the couch potato rats.

Diamond summarized her findings by saying,

"It's as simple as use it or lose it."[8]

### hopelessly over the hill?

WHAT ABOUT THAT OLD BELIEF that after a certain age you steadily head downhill and can't expect to get any fresh brain material?

Wrong again.

Dr. Richard Davidson, Director of the Laboratory for Affective Neuroscience at the University of Wisconsin, took Diamond's findings up a notch, from the rat level to the human level. In March of 2000, Davidson stated:

"Neuroscientists believed until very recently—a year or two ago—that we are born with a certain number of neurons, and that's all we have for the rest of our life. Over the last two years we have discovered that to be false. It has now been demonstrated in humans that new neurons do grow throughout the entire life span. That is a fantastic new finding."[9]

Neuroscientists can now tangibly demonstrate this continued growth. Moreover, they say that *our brains are primed to continue learning new things as long as we live.*

There is more. Not only do new neurons appear, but also *by what we choose to do and not do, we influence which neurons grow and how much they grow.*

Davidson's brain scans indicated that new neurons emerge when new learning occurs and that the parts of the brain that get the most exercise grow. In fact, the areas of the brain that are the most used literally expand and rewire on demand.

When researchers studied various parts of the brains of Londoners, they found that the area of the hippocampus known as the *mapping area* is significantly larger in cabdrivers than in non-drivers of the same age. This finding is true not only for cabdrivers, but also for anyone who repeatedly practices a particular skill. In his work with violinists, Dr. Edward Taub, a senior scientist at the Center for Aging at the University of Alabama in Birmingham, found that the amount of cortex territory devoted to the violinists' fingers continues to expand with practice. Furthermore, the cortex of violinists actually rezones itself so that more neurons are assigned to the fingers of the left hand—the hand that violinists use to produce each distinct note—than to the right.[10]

## mental power

AS IF THIS NEWS IS NOT EXCITING ENOUGH, neuroscientists in the last decade have found increasing evidence that *we have the power to change the physiology of our own brain—for better or for worse—not only by how we act but, even more amazingly, by how we think.*

From Taub's work, Dr. Alvaro Pascual-Leone, Associate Professor of Neurology at Harvard University, knew that actual physical practice could change the brain. He wanted to push further on these findings.

Pascual-Leone wondered, "Could *mental practice* produce the same results as physical practice?" To explore this, he had one group of volunteers practice a five-finger piano exercise, and another group merely think about practicing it. As expected, actual physical practice produced changes in each volunteer's motor cortex but, to the surprise of many, mere mental rehearsal produced as big a change as the physical practice. So, not only does increased physical activity maximize brain area development, even *thinking* about it can do the job.[10]

## emotional power

IT IS ONE THING TO VERIFY that something as tangible as physical activity, whether actual or imagined, changes the contours of our brains. What about something as touchy-feely as human emotions? It has long been recognized that how we feel emotionally often carries over to how we feel physically. Further, the physiological ripples set up by our emotions are much more than skin deep. Feelings of anger do affect our hearts. Depression does affect our immune system.

Ongoing work by Drs. Davidson, Salovey, and Goleman explores emotional intelligence and our ability to change our own emotional intelligence. There is indication that when we transform our own emotions, we appear to be affecting much more than skin and organs. We may be changing the connectivity of the brain itself.[11]

## research and real life

WHAT DO THESE RESEARCH FINDINGS HAVE TO DO with your daily life? They make a big difference to someone like Steve, an entrepreneur in his early sixties. Steve came to me because he felt stuck.

"When I was young, my dad told me that I'd never amount to much. At my last job, my boss told me the same thing. Those words just keep coming up again and again in my head. I guess I'll always be a loser."

That negative brain groove was Steve's default mode. The groove was so deeply entrenched that Steve believed it was impossible to change.

I now have a clear response for Steve. I can say, with the support of scientific research,

"Steve, that loser outlook is not a life sentence. You can change that."

Of course I let Steve know that radically changing a deep groove takes time. But changing the direction of the groove can happen instantly.

As Pascual-Leone demonstrated, the brain re-wires itself based on what we do, and even on what we think. By the choices Steve makes, in response to discomfort as well as to pleasure, he can derail old non-useful habits and develop abilities that perhaps he was unable to access previously. This means that he is not hopelessly circumscribed by his earlier development or non-development.

Every time that Steve does his Cue-2-Do strategy, he sparks the shift. And the more that Steve moves in that direction by his everyday choices, the more he is guiding his brain, his body, and his emotions away from the victim groove and towards a proactive habit.

When Steve reverts back to his old I'm-a-loser mode, I encourage him to do the verb tense exercise. I ask him to make accurate temporal distinctions and to say them out loud:

"In the past, I often believed that I was a loser. . . ."

"Right now, in the present, I . . ."

Steve's grammatical clarification weakens the life-sentence power of his old belief and resets his wiring to the new direction.

## but sometimes it's really hard

I KNOW FROM EXPERIENCE how difficult it is to change deeply-entrenched habits. Sometimes it seems nearly impossible. At those times the research of Dr. Jeffrey Schwartz, Research Professor at the UCLA School of Medicine, gives me hope.

Schwartz conducted groundbreaking work with a supremely challenging group, patients with OCD (Obsessive-Compulsive Personality Disorder). Individuals with OCD find it notoriously difficult to change behavior patterns even when their rational self recognizes that their actions, such as frequent hand-washing or repeated checking to make sure that switches are off, are both counterproductive and unnecessary. Dr. Schwartz demonstrated that it is possible for people with OCD to change very deeply ingrained patterns of behavior by *using their brains in a different way*. Schwartz discovered something else: when his patients changed their behavior, they changed their brains as well. And when they changed their brains, that served in turn to change their behavior.

Schwartz's success with OCD patients led him to affirm that *every adult has the ability not only to grow new neurons, but also the capacity to repair damaged neurons and change the function of old ones*.

This is indeed an astounding reality. How you act, what you choose to do or not do, even how you think and what you think, can and does change the very physiology of your brain. In *The Mind and the Brain: Neuroplasticity and the Power of Mental Force*,

Schwartz and science writer Sharon Begley state that:

> "the power of willful activity to shape the brain remains the working principle not only of early brain development, but also of brain function as an ongoing, living process."[12]

## the brain and the OASIS Strategies

SCHWARTZ AND BEGLEY'S PHRASE, *willful activity*, is the key to the OASIS Strategies.

Every instant of your life you face multiple choices. At each decision point, you either remain in a familiar pattern or you opt for a new route. If you continue in the familiar, you strengthen, for better or for worse, the wiring of this habit. If you select an alternate route, you can reinforce—even *create*—a groove/attitude/habit that moves you towards more vibrant health.

Remember Steve? If he is in his loser mode and is unaware that he's there, most likely he will stay there; in so doing, he is buttressing his loser wiring.

If Steve sharpens his awareness by using a Cue-2-Do, he can recognize what channel he is on. When he does this, he is able to pinpoint which wiring he is charging. He then has the option of continuing to charge that wire or of choosing a different channel. When he deliberately switches modes, he stops feeding the loser wiring and pitches his power to an alternate route. Every time Steve consciously chooses or willfully acts, he has the possibility of jump-starting, quite tangibly, his own health.

The OASIS Strategies are extremely portable and eminently practical tools to wire your brain towards balance, towards health, towards sanity.

Whenever you take willful action, whenever you:

- calm yourself in a chaotic situation by focusing on a stone and breathing,
- catch yourself in poor-me and consciously switch to can-do,
- intercept an angry knee-jerk response with a three-breath countdown, or
- spot your body's fatigue and relieve it with a Four-Directions stretch,

you are in fact directing the wiring of your brain away from dis-ease and towards balance. You are pulling away from depleted functioning to move towards efficient energy usage. You are giving yourself refuge and pleasure. You are creating an oasis in the overwhelm.

### old dogs, new tricks

WHOEVER SUBSCRIBES TO THE NOTION that you can't teach an old dog new tricks hasn't met my mother-in-law Miriam.

Two weeks before her eighty-ninth birthday, we asked Miriam what she would like for the big day. She replied, "Aw, nothing. I really have everything I need. Just your love is plenty."

A week later, Miriam phoned.

"You know, I've been thinking. A lot of my friends out here have computers and they send email to their grandchildren. I've been talking with them and thinking about it and researching it. I don't think I really need a whole computer shebang. I think one of those Web TV keyboards I can just hook up to the TV that I already have will do it. But don't go to any trouble."

We researched and found out that Miriam was right. We picked up what she wanted at Circuit City and went to her place on her birthday to hook up the Web TV.

Miriam got down to business immediately. She sat her 4'11" frame down in her favorite chair, experimented with the keyboard, asked for help a few times, and then sent off her first two emails: one to Josh, her eldest grandchild out in Oakland, and one to my sister Mary in the Philippines. She smiled up at us:

"Isn't that amazing? And to think they'll have my letters before we finish eating dinner!"

Next day the now eighty-nine-year-old Miriam phoned us.

"I'm so tickled with your birthday present. I've been sending out more letters, and Josh and Mary already answered me."

When you have an *attending brain* like Miriam's, age is no deterrent. Dr. Taub reported that his most dramatic finding was the discovery that in people who take up the violin, the computer, or any skill— even at age forty or older—he found evidence of brain reorganization.[13]

Miriam knew what she wanted. She exercised charming willful activity to go after it, get it, and enjoy it.

Who knows? If Taub scanned Miriam's brain, he might find that the email-sending area of her brain is expanding even as I write.

## total balance

"It ain't over till it's over."[14]

Yogi Berra, again

EVEN TODAY I LOSE TRACK of the big picture. I focus on what's going wrong—with me, my family, my friends, the world—and I get depressed thinking about it. I wake up in the morning worried about how I'll ever finish everything I have to do that day. I get caught up in little stinky events. I don't make time to take care of myself or to enjoy the people around me.

But I'm much better now than I used to be before that life-changing July day.

My bicycle accident clearly upset the speedy, slightly tipsy balance I had established for myself. The unanticipated pothole left me with three cranial fractures, a ruptured kidney and multiple lacerations. It also gave me the opportunity to change my life.

The seventeen stitches around my left eye are barely visible now. But the numb place above my lip is still a very present reality.

That numb spot is a reminder for me. Ironically, when I slip into my speedy, unaware mode, that numb spot brings me back to feeling. I touch it to remind myself that I'm right here, right now, still alive. It lets me know that now is all I have. And that's plenty.

Honing a new pattern, whether it be emotional or physiological, is a process. Be patient with yourself as you add the OASIS Strategies to your life. Like switching from an old tennis serve to a new one, the change does not happen overnight. But nature is on your side in this process. It *wants* you to be healthy. Trees bend towards light, dandelions grow up through cracks in sidewalks, your stubbed toes and scraped knees heal.

In his work with wounded soldiers in World War I, Dr. Kurt Goldstein was surprised to find that even a severely-damaged brain worked out ways to recover its basic functions.[15] Eight decades later Ilana Rubenfeld echoed Goldstein's finding by saying,

"All people have a natural capacity for self-healing and self-regulation." Rubenfeld adds, "The ultimate responsibility for change rests with each individual person."[16]

As you practice the OASIS Strategies, you will notice that some are easier for you than others, that some situations pose more of a challenge than others.

Pay attention to your successes.

Be kind to yourself as you face your own difficulties.

NEAR THE BEGINNING OF THIS BOOK I promised that you would not need to make radical changes to your life—like moving to Hawaii or joining a monastery —to create your own oases. However, as you stop every once in a while during the day to take these sixty-second breaks, you may discover that you want to make some major changes.

Perhaps you'll recognize that you really want to spend more time with your family, or with yourself, or with a passion that you've let fall by the wayside. Or you might realize that you really want to do something specific to make your neighborhood or world a bit better.

Pay attention to what you become aware of as you do the Strategies. Maybe you'll realize that you are ready to do that next thing, whatever it may be, rather than waiting "till I have time."

Psychologists say that it takes approximately twenty-eight days to develop a new habit.[17] I usually suggest to my workshop participants that they do each Strategy as often as they brush their teeth. For most people, that's about three times a day.

So how much time will it take for you to change your brain, change your life? If you do the math, it's:

4 one-minute strategies 3 x a day =

12 minutes a day

12 minutes a day x 6* days a week =

72 minutes a week

12 minutes a day x 28 days =

336 minutes or 5.6 hours a month

Not a bad investment.

*I suggest that you allow yourself a Sabbath even for the practice of the OASIS Strategies. If you *feel* like doing the Strategies seven days a week, go ahead and do them. But don't make them one more burden that you force yourself to carry every day of the week. The point is to *enjoy* your oases.

SO NOW YOU HAVE IT: four Strategies designed to move you towards balance in your busy world.

You know by now that total balance involves your complete self: physical, intellectual, emotional and spiritual. You have experienced that what you do positively or negatively in one domain automatically affects the other domains.

The four OASIS Strategies invite you to focus on one domain at a time. And when you give attention to one area, you are benefitting your entire self. As Rubenfeld writes:

> "The body, mind, emotions and spirit are part of a dynamically interrelated system. . . Essentially, every time a change is introduced at one level of a person's being, it has a ripple effect throughout the entire physical, emotional, mental and spiritual system, changing the equilibrium of the whole person."[18]

*OASIS* offers you simple, doable ways to change your equilibrium.

You're the person in charge.

You can create oases in your busy life.

You can't stop all the overwhelm but you can live so that it does not overwhelm you.

## wall street and ancient tibet

YOU *CAN* TRAIN YOUR BRAIN to move away from craziness and towards sanity. It's all in what you choose to do with your energy. Ancient eastern wisdom coincides with western research and practicality on this important matter. In a 2002 *Wall Street Journal* article, science writer Sharon Begley wrote:

"The brain allocates neural real estate depending on what we use most. In terms of which neural circuits endure and enlarge, you can call it survival of the busiest."[19]

That same year Tenzin Gyatso, the fourteenth Dalai Lama, said:

"Happiness is not a fixed characteristic, a biological set point that will never change. Instead, the brain is plastic, and our quota of happiness can be enhanced through mental training."[20]

It is my deep hope that *OASIS* will encourage you to develop those parts of your brain and of your whole being that will bring you greater health, more vibrant happiness. That's the best kind of balance in this busy world.

You have time.
You're right here, right now.
That's enough.

# acknowledgments

I THANK MY FAMILY, FRIENDS, AND COLLEAGUES for pointing me towards oases when I'm overwhelmed. To my dear Bloom family—Paul, Josh, Noah, the memory of Miriam, and to Jesse Sugarmann: deep appreciation for your unique sparks. To my blood sisters and brothers, Jean, Rose, Mary, Rich, Vince and John, thanks for keeping alive the homegrown wisdom of mom and dad.

Warm gratitude to the many compañeros Latinos who helped me rediscover music and passion in my six years in Latin America and Europe. My coach clients, workshop participants, Chautauqua Institution students, Rubenfeld Synergy and EMDR colleagues, Clínica Hispana coworkers, *Women's Power* and *Sing it!* graduates, you give me delight. I am greatly indebted to all of you for adding to the practicality of my knowledge and the richness of my life.

Lynda Ashby Ludy, agent extraordinaire, thank you for shining your light on this book and on me. Jane Baron Rechtman, those suppers and phone chats were priceless: you're the best friend I could ask for. Cookie Polan, Sonje Williams, Bernie Coyne, Lexi Johnson, Kate Smalley, Samson Ah-Fu Chow, and John Holland, your enthusiasm and practical advice kept me balanced.

Thanks to Carol Brown and Seth Godfrey at the New Haven Free Public Library, to Lenny Yanavich and the crew at Rimage, and to Don, Kik and Ro at Tyco Copy for your ever-ready assistance and good humor. Joe FitzGerald and Alice Schumacher, here's to more bike rides.

Tony Rescigno, Gar Rowbotham, Janet Testa, Patti Scussel, Betsy Herlihy, Tony Rossley and all at the Greater New Haven Chamber of Commerce, your support buoyed me. For input on various drafts, I thank Karen Baar, Lynn Fredricksen, Suzanne Grenager, Phil Haskell, and Peter Yacavone.

Joy Bush, your photos have graced *The New York Times*, *The Village Voice*, *Connecticut Review*, and many other publications. I am pleased that they add beauty and whimsy to this book.

A very special appreciation to my teachers Ilana Rubenfeld, Thich Nhat Hanh, Jon Kabat-Zinn, Francine Shapiro, and my Indonesian guide Lous Verdier Reyerse. Your wisdom continues to brighten my daily life.

# words for the journey

HERE IS WISDOM from people I've met—in person, except for Mark Twain—along the way. May their words give you cheer.

"What shines for you? Go for that!"
Ilana Rubenfeld

"Yesterday is history. Tomorrow is a mystery. Today is a gift. That's why we call it the present."
sent to me by my little sister Jeanie

"If you don't want people to get your goat, keep your goat where they can't get it."
my mother, Bernadine Dudine Grenough

"Every life should have a little mishigas."
Seth Godfrey, my neighbor and librarian

"It's probably a blessing in disguise."
my mother, again

"Keep on pedaling."
Maria Tupper,
my Friday morning sitting companion

"Go out there and do it—with all your heart. People out there are pulling for you. They want you to be good."

> Grammy-award-winning Bobby McFerrin to all of us in his 1987 Omega workshop

"Breathing in, I calm my body. Breathing out, I smile."                                    Thich Nhat Hanh

"Worrying is like paying interest on a loan that may never come due."                      Mark Twain

"If you can't make love, make lunch."

> volleyball buddy Roger Uihlein

## OASIS Strategies: summary

On the following four pages you will find a step-by-step guide for each of the OASIS Strategies. Keep this guide nearby—in your car, at your office, on your kitchen counter—any place where you are likely to need some quick, simple strategies to balance your busy world.

# 4-D = Four-Directions

stretch your body

1. Stand up.

2. Feel your connection to the earth.

3. Stretch your arms and whole body *north* to the heavens. Say out loud the *north-south-east-west* words as you do each action.

4. Bend down—*south*—to the earth.

5. Stand again.

6. Stretch to the *east*—as far as you can.

7. Stretch to the *west*. Scan the total horizon.

# 3-B-C = Three-Breath-Countdown
## calm your mind

1. Stop the whirl. Wherever you are, give yourself some psychic space. Put both hands on your belly.

2. *Preventive*: begin with an inhale. Take in something pleasurable.

3. *Emergency*: begin with an exhale. Let go of anger, worry, agitation. Make room for calmness.

4. Take three deep breaths, slowly, gently.

5. Give yourself time to enjoy the slow-down.

# Cue-2-Do

## change your brain

When you're upset or angry, notice exactly where you feel it in your body or mind. Then ask yourself the five questions:

1. What is my cue right now?

2. What is that cue signaling: what channel am I on?

3. What's the current drama on that channel?

4. Is there anything I can do and want to do right now about the situation?

5. What action is best for me right now? Make a conscious choice. Take definite action.

# 1 Stone

## balance your total self

1. Take a stone—or any object. Hold it in your hand.

2. With your eyes open, breathe in and out, slowly, ten times.

3. Allow space for your mind to do the rinse cycle.

4. Let in the larger picture.

5. Enjoy your oasis.

# notes

## chapter 1: the overwhelm

1. Robert M. Sapolsky, *Why Zebras Don't Get Ulcers: An Updated Guide to Stress, Stress-Related Diseases, and Coping* (New York: W. H. Freeman & Co., 1998): 16.
2. Dr. Afton Hassett and Leonard Sigal, Robert Wood Johnson Medical School, quoted in "Our Bodies, Our Fears" by Geoffrey Cowley, *Newsweek* (February 24, 2002): 44.
3. Sapolsky: 13.

## chapter 3: your story: personal prep

1. M. Matteson and J. Ivacevich, *Controlling Work Stress* (San Francisco: Jossey Bass, 1987).

## chapter 4: OASIS: 60-second strategies

1. Jon Kabat-Zinn, founder of The Center for Mindfulness in Medicine, Health Care, and Society at the University of Massachusetts Medical School (www.umassmed.edu/cfm). See also Kabat-Zinn's *Full Catastrophe Living: Using the Wisdom of Your Body and Mind to Face Stress, Pain, and Illness*, book and cassettes (New York: Delta, 1990), and *Wherever You Go, There You Are: Mindfulness Meditation in Everyday Life*, book and cassettes (New York: Hyperion, 1995).
2. Heraclitus, 540-480 B.C., also said: "Everything flows and nothing stays. . . . You can't step twice into the same river."
3. From Edgar Dale's "Cone of Learning," *Audio-Visual Methods in Teaching*, 3rd ed. (Austin, TX: Holt, Rinehart and Winston, 1969).
4. Numerous studies correlate physical activity, carried out with appropriate consciousness, to improved physical and emotional well-being. See

A. Byrne and D. Byrne's "The Effect of Exercise on Depression, Anxiety, and Other Mood States" in William Bortz's *We Live Too Short and Die Too Long* (New York: Bantam, 1991), and *Harvard Medical School Health Information Bulletin* (Winter 2003): 2.1, and *Johns Hopkins Medical Letter* (February 2003): 6, for fuller descriptions.

5. Ilana Rubenfeld, *The Listening Hand: Self-Healing through the Rubenfeld Synergy Method of Talk and Touch* (New York: Bantam Books, 2000): 81.

6. Daniel Goleman in *Destructive Emotions: How Can We Overcome Them?* by the Dalai Lama and Daniel Goleman (New York: Bantam Books, 2003).

7. Yogi Berra, *The Yogi Book: "I Really Didn't Say Everything I Said!"* (New York: Workman Publishing, 1998): 95.

8. Herbert Benson and Miriam Z. Klipper, *The Relaxation Response* (New York: Harper-Torch, 1976), and Herbert Benson and William Proctor, *Beyond the Relaxation Response: How to Harness the Healing Power of Your Personal Beliefs* (New York: Berkley Publishing Group; reprint edition, 1994). Numerous sports figures vouch for the effectiveness of focused meditation in improving their games. Read professional basketball coach Phil Jackson's *Sacred Hoops: Spiritual Lessons of a Hardwood Warrior* (New York: Hyperion, 1995) for intriguing accounts with his Chicago Bulls team.

## chapter 5: staying afloat in tough times

1. Vera Gibbons, "Working: High Anxiety," printed in *Smart Money* (July 2000).

2.  Teresa Caulin-Glaser, "Complementary Medicine and Cardiac Rehabilitation for Women," *Women's Health Research at Yale Newsletter* (Winter 2003): 5.

3.  Study led by Jonathan Steinberg, Chief of Cardiology at New York's St. Luke's-Roosevelt Hospital Center, cited in "Our Bodies, Our Fears" by Geoffrey Cowley, *Newsweek* (February 24, 2002): 47.

4.  Cited in "Our Bodies, Our Fears" *Newsweek* (February 24, 2002): 48.

5.  See Sapolsky's *Why Zebras Don't Get Ulcers* for more about this on-guard state. Francine Shapiro's description of the symptoms of trauma provide fascinating insights into the hyper-alert state and how to move through it; refer to Francine Shapiro's *Eye Movement Desensitiz-ation and Reprocessing* (New York: The Guilford Press, 2nd edition, 2001) and www.emdria.org.

6.  Early twentieth-century statistics from the United States Department of Health and Human Services, Center for Disease Control and Prevention, *Morbidity and Mortality Weekly Report* 48.29 (July 30, 1999). Twentieth and twenty-first century figures from Center for Disease Control, National Center for Health Statistics, National Vital Statistics System, "Deaths, Percent of Total Deaths, and Death Rates for the Fifteen Leading Causes of Death: United States, 2000" (Sept. 16, 2002, LCWK2). Statistics regarding non-disease deaths from Dr. Pamela Peeke, "Pathways to Healing," Mind Matters Seminars (1997).

7.  Hans Selye was the first researcher to note that stress could cause peptic ulcers (Sapolsky, p. 353). Selye's classic works *The Stress of Life*, 2nd ed. (New York: McGraw-Hill, 1978), and *Stress With-*

*out Stress* (New York: Signet, 1975) give fuller pictures of Selye's decades of study on the physiology of stress in animals and humans.

8. Marian Diamond, Distinguished Professor of Anatomy at the University of California at Berkeley, has studied the science of the brain for decades. Her studies on the couch potato rats were done in the 1980s. Diamond's lecture "An Optimistic View of the Aging Brain" at the Annual Meeting of the American Society on Aging in San Francisco advises all to "use it or lose it"; see article in *Aging Today* (May/June 1998).

9. Richard Davidson, quoted in *Destructive Emotions: How Can We Overcome Them?* by the Dalai Lama and Daniel Goleman (New York: Bantam Books, 2003): chapter 8 "The Neuroscience of Emotion," 189.

10. For an engrossing description of the research of Taub and Pascual-Leone and studies of the London cabdrivers, see Sharon Begley's "Survival of the Busiest" in *The Wall Street Journal* (October 11, 2002): B1.

11. For more on emotional intelligence, see Davidson's work in *Destructive Emotions*, and numerous books by Daniel Goleman and Peter Salovey.

12. Jeffrey Schwartz and Sharon Begley, *The Mind and the Brain: Neuroplasticity and the Power of Mental Force* (New York: Regan Books, 2002): 130.

13. Cited in Begley's "Survival of the Busiest," *The Wall Street Journal* (October 11, 2002): B1.

14. Yogi Berra, *The Yogi Book*, 121.

15. Kurt Goldstein, *The Organism: A Holistic Approach to Biology Derived from Pathological Data in Man* (American Books, 1939; repr. Boston, MA: Beacon Press, 1963).

16. Rubenfeld, *The Listening Hand.*
17. There are various opinions on how much time it takes to establish a new habit. Jill Ammon-Wexler asserts (www.quantum-self.com), "The scientific truth established by quantum physics and modern neuroscience is: a new habit is created in a fraction of a millisecond." I recognize that the first step—changing the direction of a habit—may begin that quickly, but I go along with the more generally accepted time frame of twenty-eight days.
18. Rubenfeld, *The Listening Hand*, 15.
19. Begley, *The Wall Street Journal* (October 11, 2002): B1.
20. Dalai Lama and Howard Cutler, *The Art of Happiness: A Handbook for Living* (New York: Penguin Putnam, 1998) cited in Dalai Lama and Goleman, *Destructive Emotions*, 25. The Dalai Lama adds: "Whether one believes in religion or not, whether one believes in this religion or that religion, the very purpose of our life is happiness, the very motion of our life is towards happiness," *The Art of Happiness*, 13.

# bibliography

Albom, Mitch. *Tuesdays with Morrie: An Old Man, a Young Man, and Life's Greatest Lesson.* New York: Bantam Doubleday, 1997.

Berra, Yogi. *The Yogi Book: "I Really Didn't Say Everything I Said!"* New York: Workman Publishing, 1998.

Borysenko, Joan. *Inner Peace for Busy People: 52 Simple Strategies for Transforming Your Life.* Carlsbad, CA: Hay House, 2003.

Carlson, Richard. *Don't Sweat the Small Stuff* (series). New York: Hyperion, 1997.

Dalai Lama and Goleman, Daniel. *Destructive Emotions: How Can We Overcome Them?* New York: Bantam Books, 2003.

Geber, Sara Zeff. *How to Manage Stress for Success.* WorkSmart Series. New York: American Management Association, 1996.

Goleman, Daniel. *Emotional Intelligence: Why It Can Matter More than I.Q.* New York: Bantam Books, 1995.

_____, and Boyatziz, Richard, and McKee, Annie. *Primal Leadership: Realizing the Power of Emotional Intelligence.* Boston: Harvard Business School Press, 2002

Kabat-Zinn, Jon. *Full Catastrophe Living: Using the Wisdom of Your Body and Mind to Face Stress, Pain, and Illness* (book and cassettes). New York: Delta, 1990.

_____. *Wherever You Go, There You Are: Mindfulness Meditation in Everyday Life* (book and cassettes). New York: Hyperion, 1995.

Nhat Hanh, Thich. *Peace Is Every Step: The Path of Mindfulness in Everyday Life.* New York: Bantam Books, 1992, and many other books.

Richardson, Cheryl. *Take Time for Your Life* (book and cassettes). New York: Broadway Books, 1999.

Rubenfeld, Ilana. *The Listening Hand: Self-Healing Through the Rubenfeld Synergy Method of Talk and Touch.* New York: Bantam Books, 2000.

Salovey, Peter, Mayer, John D., and Brackett, Marc A. *Emotional Intelligence: Key Readings on the Mayer and Salovey Model.* Port Chester, NY: National Professional Resources, 2004.

Sapolsky, Robert M. *Why Zebras Don't Get Ulcers: An Updated Guide to Stress, Stress-Related Diseases, and Coping.* New York: W. H. Freeman & Co., 1998.

Schwartz, Jeffrey M. and Begley, Sharon. *The Mind and the Brain: Neuroplasticity and the Power of Mental Force.* New York: Regan Books, an imprint of HarperCollins Publishers, 2002.

Seaward, Brian Luke. *Stressed Is Desserts Spelled Backwards.* Berkeley, CA: Conari Press, 1999.

Selye, Hans. *The Stress of Life,* 2nd ed. New York: McGraw-Hill, 1978.

_____. *Stress Without Distress,* reissue ed. New York: Signet Book, 1991.

Shapiro, Francine. *Eye Movement Desensitization and Reprocessing,* 2nd ed. New York: The Guilford Press, 2001.

Siegel, Bernie. *Love, Medicine and Miracles: Lessons Learned about Self-Healing from a Surgeon's Experience with Exceptional Patients,* reissue ed. New York: HarperCollins Publishers, 1998.

_____. *365 Prescriptions for the Soul: Daily Messages of Inspiration, Hope, and Love,* Novato, CA: New World Library, 2004.

# index

MILLIE GRENOUGH
is an executive coach
and international
workshop presenter.

She is president of
Grenough LLC, a
coaching and training
organization based in
New Haven, CT, and
is an associate of the
Corporate Coaching
Center.

M. J. Fiedler, *Connecticut Post*

A former Catholic nun, Millie has worked as a community developer, waitress, ESOL (English to Speakers of Other Languages) teacher, nightclub singer, psychotherapist, clinical social worker and strategic planner. She created *Sing It!* workshops for people shy about singing and is the author of *Sing It! Learn English Through Song* (McGraw-Hill).

Millie is a Master Rubenfeld Synergist and a Clinical Instructor in Social Work of Psychiatry, Yale University School of Medicine.

Visit www.grenough.com for more information.